Dining With the Dead

A Guide To Arizona's Haunted Restaurants And Cafes

Debe Branning

AMERICAN
TRAVELER PRESS

Printed in the United States of America

ISBN 13: 978-1-58581-045-1

2017 printing

American Traveler Press
5738 North Central Avenue
Phoenix, AZ 85012
800-521-9221
www.AmericanTravelerPress.com

Cover photo courtesy of Chance Houston.
Cover and Interior Design: The Printed Page

Dedication

To all of my paranormal team members and friends, who graciously ignored their diets in order to dine with me at these fabulous culinary venues, gather many wondrous ghost stories, and encounter a spirit or two. You made it "as easy as pie."

Table of Contents

Preface

Why would a modern day restaurant be haunted, you ask? Stop and look around the building and its surroundings. With so many restaurants resurrected in older, historical structures, it's no surprise that some eateries are believed to be haunted by prior regular patrons and owners and/or murdered former inhabitants. Chances are the dining location is housed in a building that was once an old mercantile store, church, school, home, office building, or even an industrial factory. Some of the spirits haunting the main dining room came along with the history of the building.

So why are these eateries haunted? I asked several of my paranormal investigator friends what their theories were so I could share them with you. These restaurants are the places where people have gathered together over and over again for a long period of time. They have shared emotions (both good and bad) that were released to the universe, which is likely to leave a psychic imprint behind. Think about it...eating establishments are places where murders, suicides, disputes and illness flourish, as well as parties, weddings, gala balls, and personal award ceremonies.

Former restaurant owners informed me they can definitely understand why certain eateries are haunted by their previous owners. People put their whole life into operating a restaurant—not only financially, but also long hours day after day, year after year. Many of these places were hubs of social activity—where everybody met and emotions were shared. The former owners are still comfortable there and their protective energy remains in the woodwork of the structure.

Sometimes a place is haunted because of the history of the place or the land that surrounds it. The energy that remains behind might not have anything to do with the present use of the building. Time and space does not have any special meaning in the world of ghosts.

Some believe it is the elements that make a restaurant haunted. Perhaps it is the stones of its construction or maybe it is built over a quarry of underground crystals. And we all know water is a major factor in connecting with spirits as well as running a restaurant. Water is a key element, with dishwashers, rinse water, toilets, mop water, ice machines, and air-conditioning units, along with the pitcher of water sitting on each table.

And don't forget the constant supply of energy and emotion. Emotion moves the human spirit, and it can almost move the non-human spirit. The ghostly spirits have a way of affecting the world around us in their attempts to re-create the world around them.

This book was written for the adventurous seeker of the paranormal world who is on the hunt for someplace different to satisfy their dining pleasure. If you are tired of the same old uneventful restaurant or café, you now have a "spooktacular" selection of eating establishments served with a bit of "boo." Whenever you are on a road trip in Arizona, you can thumb through the pages and visit the establishments listed in the book's "menu."

Haunted restaurants, diners, and cafés make the best destinations whenever we travel. It should be no surprise that the same place that brings us happiness and joy will occasionally bring us thrills and chills. Here are fifty-six examples of Arizona's most haunted restaurants.

Disclaimer: Before you travel to some of the locations in this book, I recommend you call ahead and verify their hours of operation, as restaurants seem to change names, ownership, and policies as often as the fresh flowers on the dining tables.

"Bone" Appetite!

MVD Ghostchasers

Referenced frequently in this book, the MVD Ghostchasers are one of the original three paranormal teams in Arizona still in operation under the same director since 1994. The team is based out of Mesa, Arizona and a second investigation team, added in 2007, is based in Bisbee, Arizona. In the group's early days, many the members were either employees, or past employees of the State of Arizona Motor Vehicle Division (MVD). In recent years, the group has expanded its membership to include valued investigators in all walks of life. Ghost hunting has become a second skin to all of them. Paranormal investigations are approached professionally and performed with integrity. The team members are experts in spirit photography, EVP, and experienced in the latest studies and technical skills necessary in the paranormal field today. Through continued research and education, the MVD Ghostchasers have earned the trust and respect from their clients and other paranormal investigators. They follow strict paranormal protocol guidelines that has made them one of the most credible and valued teams in Arizona and the United States. Several members of the team are historians, authors, lecturers, and have appeared on various reputable paranormal network programs. The leader and founder of the crew, Debe Branning, has organized investigations throughout Arizona and arranged haunted road trips around the country. The team offers paranormal workshops for interested experienced paranormal investigators, as well as beginning ghost hunters. This keeps the team busy the year around. They have been the subjects of several newspaper articles that chronical their ghostly activities and featured in magazines such as Arizona Highway Magazine and AAA's Highroad Magazine. MVD Ghostchasers have appeared on internet radio programs as well as several local TV newscasts about Arizona hauntings. They have become a favorite each year at Phoenix Comicon and have appeared on Fearnet.com's "Streets of Fear", and Travel Channel's "Ghost Stories" and "Deadly Possessions". The team works as partners with several paranormal investigative teams in Arizona and other parts of the United States.

Cochise County

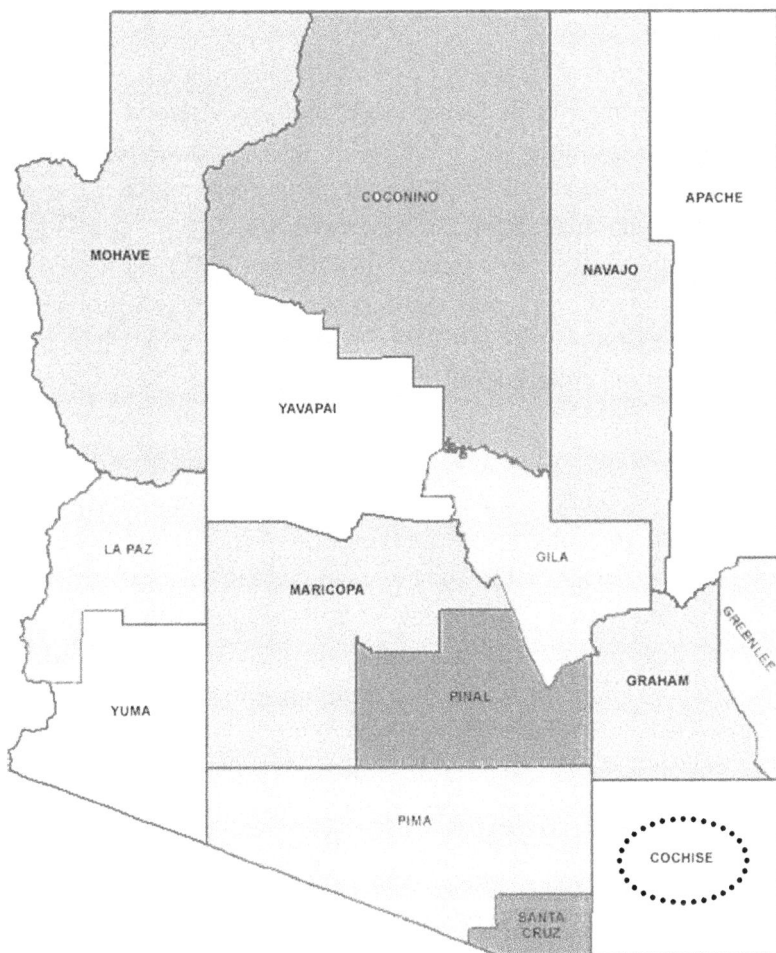

Horseshoe Café, Benson

History

The Horseshoe Café is located along Highway 80, which runs through the main business section of Benson, Arizona. The two-story stucco building was built in 1914. The structure has been used as a post office, a train depot, a bus stop, and is presently utilized as a popular eating establishment.

The café has been a Benson tradition since 1938. Travelers driving east and west on the old southern Arizona highway dubbed the "Broadway of Avenues" often stop there to rest, savor a hot meal, and enjoy good conversation.

Ghosts

Many residents in Benson believe the old landmark is haunted. Some say if you look up to the windows of the second floor, you might see an image of a ghostly woman peering back down at you. The grandmother of Ray Whaley lived in the upper apartment with her pet dog. She died alone upstairs in the rooms that overlook the highway. When the café was temporarily vacant, a passersby claimed they heard a phantom dog barking from the second floor.

A waitress recalled hearing of other staff and customers seeing a shadowy figure of an older person walking in the back hallway near the restrooms. Other staff members have reported seeing an elderly woman near the bottom step railings that lead to the upstairs living quarters. The staff of the Horseshoe affectionately refers to their ghost as "Mabel."

I spoke with a longtime Benson resident who came to the Horseshoe to have dinner with three of her good friends. They were seated at a table in the Palomino Room. This is a large dining area positioned near the bar and that faces the notorious haunted back staircase. She and her three guests studied the menu and placed

their orders with their waitress. Suddenly, the glass on the table top where they were seated cracked and shattered right in front of them. The startled diners were so frightened of what they had witnessed that they stood up and moved back into the main dining room. This same guest acknowledged that one of the owners of the café admitted there have been several unexplained occurrences in the building. Restaurant items often move from one place to another. Footsteps and voices are frequently heard with no real explanation.

Step inside the Horseshoe and you will be transported back to the days when a good home-cooked meal was part of your daily traveling adventure. Enjoy the Vern Park paintings on the walls and the huge lighted neon horseshoe adorning the ceiling. Put some coins in the jukebox and slide over in your booth. You just might have a ghostly traveler joining you for dinner or a cup of coffee. With a little luck you just might encounter a ghost at the Horseshoe Café in Benson, Arizona.

The Horseshoe Café & Bakery
154 E 4th St.
Benson, AZ 85602
520-586-2872

Copper Queen Café and Saloon, Bisbee

History

The Copper Queen Hotel began construction in 1898, and was completed in early 1902 when Bisbee was hailed as the world's largest copper mining town. The Phelps Dodge Corporation funded the construction of the five-story brick hotel, both to provide lodging for potential investors they hoped to lure into their mining operations, and to establish locations for essential local businesses. The Copper Queen hosted travelers, mining executives and politicians such as Arizona Governor George W. P. Hunt.

Known as one of the classiest hotels west of St. Louis, the hotel needed to find a way to feed its guests, too. In February of 1902, the Copper Queen Dining Room, which would be soon called the Copper Queen Café, had beautiful lighting and a seating capacity of seventy-eight persons. In the rear of the dining room were two private dining areas for families or private parties where thirty-six plates could be laid. The dining room was one of the most cheerful and attractive eating establishments to be seen anywhere in the Southwest.

The *Bisbee Daily Review* stated, "The china and silverware was all of special design having a monogram of the hotel on every piece. The glassware in the buffet was composed of a selection of the very rare and some of unusual design. Every piece was cut glass with the monogram "C.Q." etched upon it and many designs have never been used in any hotel before. The silver wine coolers were also of unique design."

The pantry was furnished with modern appliances including steam dishwashing machinery, which was entirely novel. Water, steam and air washed and dried the dishes—not even a towel was applied. The coffee urns in which the coffee was made used steam as well as other up to date appliances. Much of the cooking was done by steam. The pastry room was equipped with Burton's improved bake ovens that looked very much like steam boilers. There were several long refrigerators beside a large cold storage plant that was placed in the kitchen where meat, eggs, etc. could stay fresh for long periods of time. The first dinner served at the Copper Queen Hotel was on Monday, February 10, 1902.

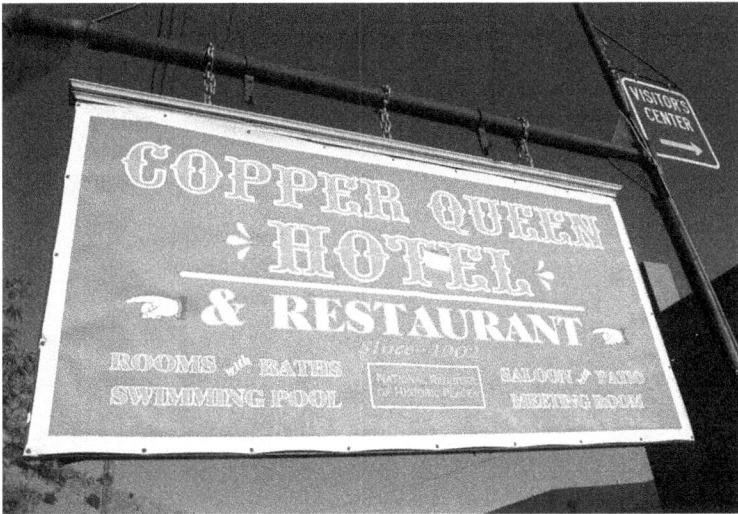

Ghosts

Several years ago, the MVD Ghostchasers spent the day exploring many of the most haunted locations in Bisbee. One of the scheduled stops was the Copper Queen Hotel. Our host was former general manager Scott Smith, who took us on a grand tour of the old hotel from top to bottom. Smith told the group about an incident he had personally witnessed in the dining room of the Copper Queen Café. A young family was having breakfast together when their young daughter quit eating her meal and became interested in something underneath the next table. Like any child, she began to fidget and tried to climb down from her seat, telling her parents that she wanted to go play with the little boy. Her parents looked around the dining room and saw no other children in the room.

"What little boy?" they asked as their daughter crouched down to the floor on her hands and knees.

"The little boy under the table!" the young girl pointed. There was no boy in sight. Could this mischievous young lad be the notorious "Billy" who is said to haunt the Copper Queen Hotel? Billy loves to play pranks on the guests and enjoys an opportunity to play with some of the visiting children. Some say Billy's mother was a waitress in the hotel dining room or perhaps a domestic in the hotel. Legends say Billy was about 8 or 9 years old when he drowned in the nearby San Pedro River. Presumably, his spirit found its way back to the hotel because his mother worked there.

Another couple came to enjoy their dinner at the Copper Queen Café after a long day of touring the mine, searching for antiques on Main Street, and enjoying the sights of Bisbee via a jeep tour. They finished their meal and the wife placed her crumpled, dirty napkin on the table next to her plate. She and her husband, along with several other bewildered guests seated at the nearby tables, watched in disbelief as the napkin smoothed itself flat again and moved to the other side of the table.

The front desk of the Copper Queen faces towards the entrance of the café. One of the front desk clerks has seen a reddish-brown-haired, solid, pink apparition of a young woman in her early twenties from the waist up. Her hair was piled high on her head in a bun, and she was wearing one of those early 1900's era high collar white blouses. Is this the ghostly waitress who refolds the napkins and sets the dining room tables?

This same front desk employee occasionally heard the footsteps of a woman walking through the dining room floor and the swooshing sound of her long skirt dragging across the room after the restaurant was closed.

Some of the Copper Queen Hotel staff has seen a shadow-like figure walking back and forth near the entrance of the Copper Queen Café—again after the restaurant is closed down for the evening and it is dark inside. It resembles a male figure, and nobody has been able to see any details of his face or stature. Perhaps he is the same gentleman the café servers have seen relaxing in a chair in the far left corner of the restaurant, puffing on what appears to be a fine cigar.

The Copper Queen Hotel keeps a diary of ghostly encounters at the front desk for guests to read. The hotel has been featured on several of the TV paranormal shows such as "Ghost Hunters" and "Ghost Adventures," and it is one of the prime locations for local paranormal conventions. Check in, enjoy the fresh clean air, and partake in a meal with some of Bisbee's "resident" diners.

Copper Queen Café
11 Howell Avenue
Bisbee, AZ 85603
520-432-2216
www.copperqueen.com

The Grand Café, Douglas

History

During MVD Ghostchasers' many adventures to Douglas, Arizona to stay at the haunted Gadsden Hotel, we found a local eating establishment noted to be equally haunted. Down the street from the Gadsden, we discovered the friendly atmosphere of the Grand Café and Gallery. It is a small quaint Mexican/American restaurant housed in one of the original buildings along "G" Avenue and just the ticket when you are visiting so close to the border.

Ghosts

Soon after one of our frequent visits, we decided to ask members of the staff if they ever felt a ghostly presence in the building. The owner at the time, Vanesa Serrano Quintana, sat down to have a chat with the MVD Ghostchasers team at dinner. Vanesa was very enchanting. She was a beautiful Hispanic woman who turned her little café into a shrine dedicated to the late Marilyn Monroe. Marilyn's likeness decorated the walls in photographs above each booth and anywhere else there was room to hang a picture or display a Marilyn doll. Vanesa even enjoyed dressing up like her idol on Halloween and for parades in Douglas.

At the time of our visit, Vanesa and her husband lived in the apartment above the café. Her encounter with the ghost happened in the wee hours of the morning. She had lit several candles around their bedroom before turning down the lights and climbing into bed. During the night, a small gust of wind blew through an open window and knocked one of the lighted candles to the floor. A throw rug began to smolder, and smoke soon filled the bedroom.

Vanesa said she was suddenly awakened by someone shaking her shoulders. She heard a man's voice say *"Wake up! Put out the fire!"* At first she thought it was her husband, but when she glanced in his direction, he was still sound asleep. Vanesa sprung from the bed and saw the small rug burning. She was able to stomp out the fire before it grew into an infernal disaster. She believed a ghost from the café protected her and the building housing the cafe.

Vanesa invited us back after closing to do an investigation of the restaurant. We explored the upstairs attic that was primary used for restaurant storage. Employees in the café were hesitant to go down in the basement, but were more than happy to open the cellar door for us to explore its primitive walls. One employee said he heard a woman singing in the basement on the day he ventured below to get kitchen supplies. He never went to the basement again. We decided to set up our recording devices in the reportedly haunted basement area. Cameras were focused on the wooden stairs and a far corner of the dark cellar where voices were heard.

The following morning, we walked over to the café from the Gadsden Hotel to collect our cameras and recording devices. We listened to silence on the recorder for the longest period of time. Finally, the recording device played back what we came for. The time stamp read 2:00 AM. The old building seemed to come alive. The recorders picked up loud noises coming from the café floor above the basement. It sounded like tables and chairs were being moved or dragged about the building. This went on for almost an hour, and then the recorder fell silent again.

Vanesa told us later the staff often found the furniture rearranged in the morning. Sometimes the dining table candles were positioned as though someone had inspected and snuffed them out for the night. Was it a ghost, or just one of Vanesa's guardian angels protecting her and the café? We know with Marilyn's likeness present everywhere in the building, "some like it hot." but not the protective spirit of the Grand Café.

Grand Café and Gallery
1119 G Avenue
Douglas, AZ 85608
520-364-2344

Daisy Mae's Steakhouse, Sierra Vista

History

The Daisy Mae's/Stronghold building is one of, if not the oldest, buildings of Cochise County in Southern Arizona. The location began as a trading post in the early 1870's. Later it served as a U.S. Post Office, a busy general store, and even a stop on the stagecoach line. In the late 1800's the building housed a brothel that catered to the soldiers stationed nearby at Fort Huachuca. It began its current status as a restaurant in the early 1940's. There were a series of different restaurant businesses housed in the large adobe building, the most famous being G & M Stronghold, until Daisy Mae's took the reins in 1993. Daisy Mae's won a service award as one of the top twenty-five steakhouses in America from the American Academy of Restaurants and Steakhouses

Mesquite grilled entrees are the specialty of the house and the steaks are the finest in Arizona. Ribs, chicken, pork, fish and a variety of Angus Beef steaks are all on the menu.

As you walk into the building, you will be greeted near the bar and escorted to one of the many dining areas. There is a banquet area for that special family celebration, quiet tables and booths in separate dining areas. Or booths near the bar where you can enjoy music and good company. If you want to be spooked while you dine at Daisy Mae's, ask to be seated in the infamous "Charlie's Room."

Ghosts

MVD Ghostchasers Debe Branning, Kenton Moore, Chris and Shiela Mc Curdy, Mark Christoph and Brenda McIntyre all met for dinner at Daisy Mae's Steakhouse in August 2008. Debe immediately asked to be seated in "Charlie's Room" so they could be near the reportedly haunted area of the building in hopes of a Charlie encounter.

Charlie is said to have been one of the loyal patrons that frequented the facility when it was the brothel. It was conveniently within walking distance near the Main Gate of the Fort. Charlie was standing near the bedrooms or "cribs" in the brothel one evening when a knife fight erupted over the virtue of one of the ladies. Charlie was fatally stabbed and murdered. He was found dead on the floor near one of the ladies' rooms.

It is said Charlie's ghost has been present in the building ever since. Numerous sightings and incidents have been reported through the years.

Debe headed over to chat with the wait staff to gather some of the ghost stories they had heard or personal experiences encountered. Some of the ladies were happy to share their ghost tales.

"I was here after closing one night," Pam began, "I was alone in the banquet room—yet I didn't feel like I was really alone. I had gone back there to put away some sugar in the supply area. All of a sudden I felt like I had walked into a thick spider web. I tried to brush it off, but there was nothing there. Then all of a sudden I felt very cold and the hair on my arms stood straight up!"

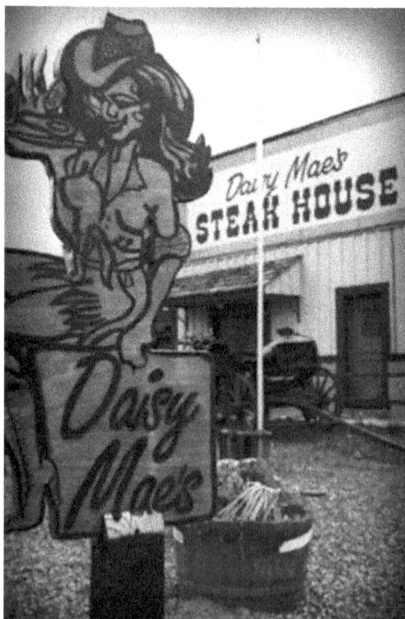

Another waitress escorted Debe to one of the back dining areas to show her where some of the doors to the cribs once stood.

"There were doors going to the bedrooms where this wall is now," the young lady stated and pointed to the bricked up entrances of old doorways. There was also a set of bedrooms on the other side of the building."

Debe snapped a photo of the filled in brickwork. Only a faint outline of the old doorways could be seen.

"Oh!" the young lady continued. "I learned a story about the building that was very interesting. Follow me."

Debe followed the girl to a section of the restaurant where one needs to step down to another level of the dining area that leads towards the banquet area.

"When they were remodeling the building the owner found a tunnel under this stairway," she smiled, "They say the soldiers from the Fort used the tunnel as a getaway when their wives came looking for them here at the brothel. The wives would come in, look around, and when there was no sign of their man, they headed back home feeling a false sense of relief."

Debe scurried back to the dining table where the MVD Ghostchasers were finishing up their steak dinners. She pried Chris, Kenton and Mark from their seats to show them what she had just learned.

A few more photos were snapped in the area near the bedrooms where Charlie met his demise. The dark area near some of the exposed old bedrooms made one think Charlie would be in view at any moment.

Debe spoke with Cherish, who is one of the owners of Daisy Mae's and asked her about her experiences with Charlie's ghost.

"My father use to see him all the time in that area we call Charlie's Room," Cherish told me, "But, I have only seen him a few times myself."

"What did he look like?" Debe was very curious. Sometimes ghosts are merely stories, but in this case there has been a witness to his appearances.

"Well," she took a deep breath, "He has long hair. He wears a flannel type shirt and always has on baggy pants."

"Is he always in the same area over near Charlie's Room?" Debe asked.

"Yes, always in that section of the building," Cherish confirmed, "And then he simply walks away and disappears into the wall."

Whether Charlie was a soldier or an ordinary man who came to the brothel to seek his pleasures, we do not know. March on into Daisy Mae's Steakhouse some night when you are visiting Sierra Vista or the Fort Huachuca area. Be seated for dinner in one of the brothel cribs and keep a watchful eye out for Charlie…and that's an order!

Author's note: Daisy Mae's Steak House closed in 2014. The historic building is still standing, but no longer serving steaks and spirits at this time.

Daisy Mae's Steak House
332 N Garden Avenue
Sierra Vista, AZ 85635
520-452-8099
www.daisymaessteakhouse.com

Café Margarita aka Nellie Cashman's, Tombstone

History

An original adobe building built in 1879, Café Margarita (formerly known as Nellie Cashman's Restaurant) is known as Tombstone's oldest restaurant building. Walking through the front entryway is like stepping back in time. The dining room has high ceilings, and tall window sills have ledges where pies once cooled. There's a stone fireplace in one corner that adds warmth and comfort to the small eatery. Stained glass windows accent the period setting. Wooden floors creak as you step across the room to your table. Photos of the restaurant's namesake adorn the walls.

Nellie Cashman was a woman of good will and had an unusual spirit for her time. She spent her entire life doing good deeds for others. Her business was geared to feed hungry settlers and give them shelter if needed. She donated large sums of money to various charities in the mining towns she resided in from the fifty-cent meals she served. Nellie was affectionately known as "Angel of the Camp" for her unselfish dedication to the townsfolk. In 1880 Nellie set her eyes on the boom town of Tombstone, AZ. Nellie became a part of the rich silver mining camp long about the same time as the Earp clan and John Clum who founded the *Epitaph* newspaper. She operated a retail business selling boots and other supplies to the miners. Later she bought and became the proprietress of the Russ House. Russ House was originally a boarding house with a small restaurant. Nellie's advertisements boasted the best meals in town.

When the Tombstone silver mines began to slow down, Nellie knew it was time to move on to the next mining camp that was about to prosper. Nellie sold Russ House in 1886 and traveled on to new investments. The building remained a boarding house until the 1950's. At that time, the interior was gutted out and renovated back into a restaurant. Many believe Nellie Cashman still oversees the wait staff and guests in the popular Tombstone dining establishment that once carried her name.

One of the few remaining original buildings from the wild Tombstone boom days, the restaurant—now Café Margarita—sits on a quiet corner away from the staged gun fights in the town center and gift shops that line Allen Street. At Café Margarita, they take pride in serving their guests authentic Mexican and Italian dishes made with the finest ingredients available. Relax while sipping on an ice-cold cactus margarita.

Ghosts

The MVD Ghostchasers have held two different Spirit Photo Workshops in Tombstone. Both workshop crews made Nellie Cashman's (Café Margarita) their stop for a great homestyle dinner. Tales of ghost encounters are well received at our dinners, ideas are exchanged, and sometimes new ghost hunting partnerships are established.

The owner and wait staff of the then Nellie Cashman's were anxious to share their stories with us. Employee's feel the spirits are from the frontier days—but not necessary Nellie Cashman herself. They have witnessed a lady dressed in Victorian-style clothing in the restaurant late at night. One employee saw an older gentleman attired in an outdated black suit walk straight into the kitchen. No one was in there upon an immediate inspection. The owner has seen the apparition of a man and woman dressed in fine western clothing walk in the dining room together out of the corner of her eye. Thinking they might have been re-enactment players from town, she turned to serve them, only to find nobody there. Kitchen employees hear voices in the restaurant area after closing when the doors are locked and they know they are the only ones left in the building.

Neighbors have seen a lady coming out the back door carrying a lunch bucket as if she was setting out to deliver a meal to some hardworking miner Some people believe the woman was merely a boarder that lived on the grounds years later and was perhaps killed on the premises. Others believe the man in the patio courtyard area was also one of the boarders. Did the woman meet her death at the hands of this mysterious man? Are they are still searching for each other on the property?

The employees feel the ghosts are a playful crew for the most part. Lights mysteriously turn on and off. Some items in the restaurant get misplaced or turn up missing altogether. Objects move around the building after hours. One waitress had left some pots and pans that were to be used the following morning on top of the stove before locking up for the night. The next morning she found a different set of cookery sitting on the stove when she entered the kitchen. She chuckled, thinking about how Nellie was still in control of her kitchen.

Another morning they entered the building to find a painting that hung over the fireplace lying on the floor a good six feet from the wall. The painting was remarkably undamaged, and the frame was still intact. Upon inspection, they found the nail still secure in the wall.

The MVD Ghostchasers were invited to investigate Nellie Cashman's restaurant after hours. The crew silently gathered in the dining room of the small restaurant at 10pm. Everyone took a seat at a table and emptied their bags of equipment such as cameras, camcorders, various EMF meters, thermo scanners, and digital and tape recording devices. It was lights out except for an occasional flash of a camera. Some sat silently, trying to mentally seek the spirits and acknowledge any messages sent their way. One investigator noted high EMF readings in the hallway near the wait station. Some went outside to photograph the side patio area adjoining the restaurant. After two hours, our vigil in the silent café ended. There was a usual array of abnormalities on photos, but no late night apparitions made an appearance. Everyone agreed the spirits of the establishments were peaceful and nothing to be feared.

The owners agree. They also maintain that the ghosts may be sensitive to criticism or to nonbelievers, and that is usually when they have made themselves known. A widely circulated story is of a patron who came into the restaurant and began to ridicule and make fun of Nellie. To the diner's disbelieving eyes, a mustard bottle jumped up from the table and spilled its yellow contents all over his or her clothing.

So when you are ready for a meal that takes you south of the border, the peaceful energy of Café Margarita is the spot for your fiesta while tromping Tombstone's Allen Street. But remember, Nellie was a high-spirited frontier woman and won't think twice about keeping law and order in her restaurant, even if it means you could be "slimed" by a bottle of spicy mustard or a bowl of salsa!

Café Margarita
131 S 5th St.
Tombstone, AZ 85638
520-457-2277
www.cafe-margarita.com

Crystal Palace Saloon, Tombstone

History

The Crystal Palace Saloon opened its doors in July 1882 on the site of the charred remains of the Golden Eagle Brewing Company in Tombstone, Arizona—the town "too tough to die." The second structure included two stories, providing office space upstairs.

The saloon, back when saloons were open 24 hours a day, was known for its "honest" gambling games, and strove to keep the "upper crust folks" of Tombstone inside the swinging doors. It soon became a popular dining establishment and carried the finest wines, liquors and cigars. Virgil Earp kept his offices on the top floor of the building, as did the local physician, Dr. George E. Goodfellow, and the coroner, Dr. H.M. Matthews. It is said that "Buckskin" Frank Leslie was a night watchman at the building for a short time.

It was a very popular spot in Tombstone, and today, it continues to draw in fans of the Old West each weekend. Folks come in for a refreshing drink, food, and to listen to live music on stage. Another group of patrons known as ghost investigators stop by looking for spirits, including those not of the drinking kind. You see, some of the upstanding (and some of the not so upstanding) characters of the Old West still frequent the building.

Ghosts

Many of the employees tell stories of having seen ghostly cowboys lined up and waiting to be served at the beautiful mahogany bar. When the bartenders turn to take an order, they discover that the phantom cowhands of the Old West have simply vanished into thin air. Patrons of the saloon have witnessed ghostly pioneers sitting alone at the tables, onstage, or have seen unexplained shadows moving about in different locations near the bar.

Customers frequently report that they see an elderly man rise from a table and slowly enter the restroom or stand in the hallway near the facility. The part that puzzles most guests is the fact that the man never returns from the restroom. Employees have gone into the restroom to check on the well-dressed elderly gentleman to find absolutely nobody there. And to make things even more phenomenal, there is only one way in or out of the restroom. There is no back entrance. Where does the spirit go? Is this a portal to the other world?

Perhaps the ghostly gentleman is none other than Virgil Earp. The Crystal Palace did not see much trouble when Earp kept his office upstairs above the Crystal Palace. Some of the bartenders proclaim that if you are rude to the wait staff today, the ghost of Virgil Earp will make you think twice about ever being obnoxious again. They tell a story about a patron who was making comments to one of the waitresses and was getting a bit out of hand. At some point he headed to the bathroom, and while he was washing his hands at the sink he noticed an older, taller man dressed in period clothing standing behind him in the mirror. He spun around and found nobody there. He glanced back at the mirror just as the man behind him grabbed his arm and slammed him against the wall. The obnoxious patron ran out of the Crystal Palace and vowed never to return. Some folks say that Virgil Earp did things like that when he was alive and he just might be up to his same old escapades now. No rudeness was allowed in the Crystal Palace back in the days of the Wild West—and it is still unacceptable today.

The Crystal Palace also reports disembodied voices and phantom footsteps late at night when the bar and restaurant is closed. The old roulette wheels hanging on the walls have been known to spin on their own as if a gambling game of the past is in session.

Come in, grab a seat, and order up dinner and a sarsaparilla. Be on your best behavior unless you dare to confront the spirit of former Deputy Marshal Virgil Earp. And, keep an eye on that cowboy near the bar—or was that just the glimmer of a ghost?

Crystal Palace Saloon
436 E Allen St.
Tombstone, AZ 85638
520-457-3611
www.crystalpalacesaloon.com

Big Nose Kate's Saloon, Tombstone

History

Big Nose Kate's Saloon is housed in what was once the Grand Hotel. The original building opened on September 9, 1880 during Tombstone's heyday. The hotel was built above a silver mine shaft which runs throughout the town beneath the streets of Tombstone. Mrs. Jessie E. Brown proudly managed the luxurious hotel. Some of the famous guests who registered at the Grand were Lily Langtree, Eddie Foy, The Earps, Doc Holliday, the Clantons, and the McLaurys. This by far was the most prestigious hotel in Tombstone. It had a beautiful staircase with a black walnut banister. Costly furniture and carpeting decorated the lobby and all sixteen rooms. Expensive artwork and crystal chandeliers adorned the halls and dining room. The kitchen was built with all the modern conveniences of the time. It housed a Montagin range that was 12 feet in length, with a patent heater, hot and cold faucets, and every appliance available to feed a large crowd of patrons for dinner. Grand balls were held in the hotel for the guests and visitors. Travelers enjoyed a comfortable room upstairs and fine dining on the ground floor, and drinks were served in a saloon and German deli called the "Grotto" in the basement.

The hotel was burned by a devastating fire that destroyed most of Tombstone on May 26, 1882. The second floor and ornate staircase was gone. The beautiful apartments of the Tombstone Club in the hotel were among the first to kiss the flames. The general building of the Grand Hotel was next to meet the fiery doom; the wooden staircase on the outside of the building in the rear fell. A wooden staircase from the basement that led up to the kitchen and the spirit world was all that remained of the Grand Hotel.

Several saloons have been in operation on the site of the old hotel building. Today, Big Nose Kate's Saloon offers great food and beer on tap for visitors who want to quench their thirst in a real western bar. In business since 1985, it sports a long bar set up with mirrors on one side of the room. Tables are scattered on the main floor and there is usually live music to entertain you as you sip your cool beer or sarsaparilla. The bar is named after the notorious Kate Elder, or Big Nose Kate as she was called. Known as a con artist and prostitute, she had also gained fame as the girlfriend of Doc Holliday.

There is a store in the basement called The Shaft where you can purchase Southwestern attire and other gift items. It is also the area where you can gaze into what was once an entrance to an old mine tunnel and the spot where the ghost of "the Swamper" is said to roam. The man known as the Swamper did odd jobs around the hotel as exchange for room and board. He was a trusted and honest employee who kept his own bedroom in the dark basement of The Grand Hotel. This was his secret getaway where he enjoyed solitude and privacy away from the hotel guests. The Swamper was known to have a passion for silver. His basement quarters were deep enough below the surface of the streets to gain entrance into one of the winding mine shafts which ran underground beneath most of Tombstone. The Swamper spent many years tunneling into the mine shaft and eventually gained access to a thick vein of silver where he extracted silver nuggets. The mine entrance is still a feature of the bar that guests enjoy visiting and gazing into the deep shaft.

Ghosts

Many say the Swamper spent his secret cache of silver on pleasures throughout the town of Tombstone. Others speculate he hoarded his silver in an unknown hiding place beneath the surface of the Grand Hotel. He knew the tunnels under the hotel like the back of his hand and it would not be hard to stash his silver where no one else would find it.

Employees of Big Nose Kate's Saloon swear they have seen the ghost of the Swamper wandering the basement corridors and back stairs. Photographs have captured the ghostly image of an apparition inside the upstairs saloon. Even one of the saloon postcards carries this eerie image. It is believed the ghost of the Swamper is still protecting the hidden silver he so carefully buried on the property of the historic building.

The Big Nose Kate's web page tells a story about the time the building's owner and several employees decided to go down and explore the old Swamper's tunnel. They soon discovered that it still led all the way back into the old shafts of the Toughnut Mine. They carefully made it safely back to the basement, but just as they approached the Swamper's tunnel, they heard a load moaning sound and heavy boot steps coming down the stairs leading to the tunnel. They thought someone had entered the closed saloon, and began to search the premises, only to find the building empty and the doors locked and secured.

One of the employees told us he had experienced doors opening and closing on their own many times. He often heard noises coming from the basement that sounded like heavy boot steps and the jiggling of spurs climbing up and down the staircase. Suspecting an intruder, he would rush to the stairs hoping to catch whoever was walking around the lower level. As soon as he neared the top of the steps, the noises would cease. Disembodied voices from the basement play out like a static muffle, sounding like a radio station in a distance.

The staff at Big Nose Kate's decided the Swamper needed a more personal name so they began to call him Felix. Felix is very mischievous and likes to pull pranks on the female employees. He thinks nothing of tugging on their hair, tossing lids off the trashcans onto the floor, giving them a playful pinch on the behind, and even calling out their names.

Another haunted location in the building seems to be the closed-off balcony viewing area above the barroom and dance floor. Perched there are two mannequins dressed in 1880's period clothing. Several employees reported incidents where they have witnessed the mannequins taking human form and moving right before their eyes. They watched wide-eyed as the female mannequin inched towards the railing, leaned over and toppled down to the floor. Glancing up at the male mannequin, they saw his face turn towards to where his companion had stood. One afternoon a female employee looked up to the balcony area where the mannequins proudly watch over the tourists who enter Big Nose Kate's for a drink or a bite to eat. She spotted a beautiful ghostly woman in 1880's fashion with a parasol over her shoulder. The baffled employee watched in awe as the woman with the ringlet curls smiled and observed the people down below. She eventually faded away.

The MVD Ghostchasers were invited to stop in for an after-hours investigation of Big Nose Kate's Saloon during their Tombstone Spirit Photography Workshop in April 2006. Several of the folks attending the workshop quietly entered the building for the late night investigation. The basement area had already been closed down for the night, so one of the employees escorted the group through the kitchen and down the old wooden stairway— the only original piece of the Grand Hotel.

On the left of the stairs was the Swamper's room. It is carefully barred to protect guests from taking a tumble or getting lost in the mines. A trusted employee stood with the group after she unlocked the bars to the room so they could enter and photograph the area under her supervision. Their EMF meters immediately showed a fluctuation in the energy field in front of them. The readings moved from 1.2 to as high as 3.3 as one of the investigators noted the date, time and reading in a notebook.

With the safety bar back in place, one of the investigators placed his night vision camera lens through the bars in hopes of photographing what ever was lurking at the mine shaft entrance.

The investigators were told stories of clothing racks and displays being moved about the room, so several more photos of the basement were taken before the group headed back up to the main floor. They stopped on the old set of wooden stairs to test for EVP to see if any of the spirits had any messages to report that evening. The sensation of a cold breeze swept over the group, but no voices were recorded.

Other witnesses have claimed that apparitions of cowboys have been seen at the bar, standing in doorways, and knocking over cases of beer in the basement. Lights turn on and off by themselves, and silverware has been known to fly off the tables.

MVD Ghostchasers director, Debe Branning, led the group back upstairs for another session of photos and EVP after the last of the saloon patrons had departed and the cleanup by the staff had been completed.

Gary Tone, one of the longtime members of the group, thought he had heard footsteps in the back corner of the room and went over to investigate. He snapped a few photos that were most likely dust orbs due to the age of the building and surroundings. An employee confirmed that many times when he was cleaning up that area of the room for the night, he did not feel he was alone and often heard the same footsteps.

The team turned off the lights and sat in the near darkness of the building for almost forty-five minutes. A few EMF sweeps showed magnetic energy activity for short periods of time peaking steadily between 2.6 and 2.9. At 3:00 A.M. the few remaining employees were ready to call it a night and the workshop crew agreed. We collected our cameras from the Swamper's room and rolled up the equipment after experiencing an eventful night. The management invited the ghost hunters back to do further research some other evening in the future.

A visit to this historic structure may provide more than a lesson in Tombstone history. The history just might come to life in the form of a ghost or even a possessed mannequin.

Big Nose Kate's Saloon
417 E Allen St.
Tombstone, AZ 85638
520-457-3107
www.bignosekates.info

Coconino County

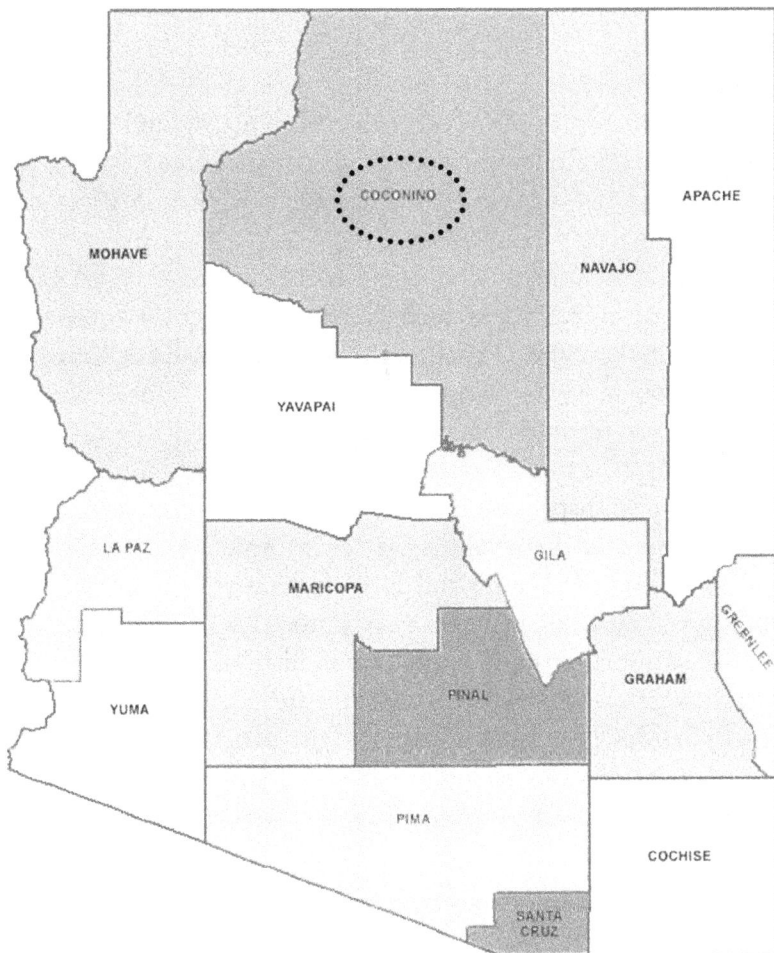

Cameron Trading Post Restaurant, Cameron

History

The Cameron Trading Post is located about fifty miles north of Flagstaff on US Route 89 and sits high on a cliff above the Little Colorado River—a tributary to the mighty Colorado River that flows through the Grand Canyon.

A one lane suspension bridge was constructed over the Little Colorado River in 1911 as the first easy access over the gorge. Two brothers, Hubert and C.D. Richardson, established the Cameron Trading Post in 1916. The post was named after Ralph Cameron, Arizona's last territorial delegate before statehood in 1912. The trading post was located on a dirt road just a few yards from the river. The new suspension bridge made it more convenient for the Richardsons and the neighboring Native American tribes. It was first visited by the Navajo and Hopi Indians who came to barter and trade their wool, blankets and livestock for dry goods.

The original structure still stands near the river. There has been several additions and modifications added through the years. Besides housing a curio and gift shop, the trading post boasts a beautifully restored dining room. The large dining facility offers a wall of large windows that overlook the Little Colorado River.

The Richardson brothers were respected and trusted by the local Native American people. The Navajo and Hopi told them stories, and they responded by translating the tales to travelers at the trading post.

Through the years, the roads improved and a new interest in tourism of the area began to grow. The Cameron Trading Post's convenient location near the Grand Canyon and other fascinating areas made it a popular stop with the early travelers as well, so an improved dining room area was much needed.

The Cameron Trading Post Restaurant is owned by the people who live in the surrounding region. Many of them have had family roots tied to the area for generations. The restaurant, open for breakfast, lunch and dinner, serves Mexican and Navajo food. They are famous for their Navajo Taco—a meal in itself!

Ghosts

The wait staff was eager to escort Cindy Lee, Susie Dwyer, Karen Marchetti and myself around the Cameron Restaurant Dining Room, where paranormal activity has been known to occur on somewhat a regular basis.

"Ghosts or what we call "shadow people" (shadowy forms of humans) have been seen walking in the dining room," one of the waitresses told us, "It usually happens near our 9pm closing time." After our delicious lunch—the Navajo Taco of course—our waitress returned to our table and offered a few more ghost stories she had gathered from other restaurant staff members working in the kitchen and in the dining room. She led us to a back dining room that was constructed as an addition to the original building in recent years.

"A few years ago there use to be a little alleyway between the restaurant and an old motel that sat across from this spot. They tore down the outdated motel and built on a new annex to the restaurant and trading post," she explained. "Now employees and guests see what looks like "transparent" people walking along this corridor where the passageway between the two buildings was. Some guests even say they have been poked or pushed aside by the large strong hands of an invisible man while being seated at one of these side tables. We have witnessed a ghost of an elderly man from the early 1900's era sitting in a chair smoking a pipe or a cigar near the doorway many times."

We noticed an old, weathered upright piano propped up along the same wall. Our waitress/impromptu guide smiled as she ran her fingers across the ivory keys.

"We have heard the piano playing a lively old dance tune on several evenings." She recalled, "But! When we come into the room to applaud the piano player, the room is always vacant. Again… this all seems to happen near closing time."

"Who do you think the ghosts are?" we asked.

The waitress seemed to think it could be the Richardsons or a former employee named Edward. Edward was a dedicated worker at the trading post and rarely missed a day of work. He never left his assigned workday tasks unfinished. Edward has passed away, but he could still be making sure everything is in order.

Another employee, Jimmy, who has worked at Cameron Trading Post for many years, told us he had heard ghost stories of a little pioneer girl who has been seen darting back and forth in front of the massive stone fireplace in the dining room. Nobody has any idea who the young girl might be. It is feared she may have drowned in the Little Colorado River during one of the floods at Tanner Crossing along the Mormon Trail. Tanner Crossing is a quarter mile from the trading post and she could be wandering the property in search of her family.

The Cameron Trading Post Restaurant is the perfect spot to take a break when traveling to and from a busy day at the South Rim of the Grand Canyon. Order a famous Navajo Taco for lunch or dinner and if you are lucky, one of the spirits of the trading post might join you. Either way, it's a pretty good tradeoff.

Cameron Trading Post
466 HWY 89
Cameron, AZ 86020
1-800-338-7385 or 1-928-679-2231
www.camerontradingpost.com

The Museum Club, Flagstaff

History

The Museum Club was built in 1931 by Dean Eldredge. As a boy he found a petrified frog in Wisconsin and it spurred a lifetime dream of becoming a taxidermist. Eldredge was an avid hunting sportsman and collector. He wanted a unique place to display his hunting trophies and vast collection of rifles and Indian artifacts. For 25 cents, people came from miles around to see his collection of strange oddities of nature. The building later became a store, trading post and taxidermy shop. Eldredge displayed his own trophies and was able to create displays for his customers.

The building was sold in 1936, after prohibition, to a Flagstaff saddle maker named Doc Williams. He turned the Museum Club into a popular off the wall night club—or roadhouse as they once called them. It was promoted as the largest log cabin in Arizona and packed in crowds of people from everywhere. It was built around five large ponderosa pines that appeared to be growing out of the dance floor. You entered the door through an inverted trunk of one of the native pine trees. There was a mahogany bar from the 1880's in the NW corner of the room. Folks coming to the Museum Club to eat and drink were mesmerized by the more than 85 mounted animals on display from the taxidermy shop days. Soon the locals nicknamed the place "The Zoo."

During the 1960's and 1970's the roadhouse was owned by Don and Thorna Scott. According to local legends, the couple both suffered tragic and untimely deaths. The Scotts lived upstairs above the establishment. One day in 1973, Thorna stood near the top the stairs and fell. She lapsed into a coma and never recovered. Don became very despondent at the loss of his dear wife, and later took his own life by shooting himself with a rifle in front of the stone fireplace.

The current owners feel the Scotts loved the Museum Club so much that their spirits frequently make a visit and mingle with the patrons and the taxidermy animals when the Zoo is busy and music is playing.

Ghosts

The staff of the Museum Club says there are sometimes footsteps and creaks heard coming from the upstairs apartment. A man who lived temporarily in the apartment told them of being pinned to the ground by an unseen force. A woman's voice told him "You only need to fear the living. Don't be afraid. Only the living can hurt you." This is a rule we ghost hunters often live by. The man was so scared he climbed out of the window as he had no desire to run down and use the front door.

The spirit of Thorna has appeared looking into the roadhouse from the back stairway. Thorna has also made appearances during the daytime in various locations of the bar and restaurant. She has been seen working at the back bar. A customer complained at the front bar about a female bartender who ignored him and refused to wait on him. The man was totally surprised when the front bar bartender served him a drink and informed him there was no one on duty at the back bar.

Other guests have seen Thorna enjoying the music as she sits alone at a table in a booth in a dark corner. Occasionally, a gentleman has seen her sitting alone and stopped at the bar to order her a drink. Upon his return to the table with drinks in hand, he finds the lady has vanished into thin air.

The bartenders have come into work to find the shelves behind the bar in disarray. Beer bottles are switched around, drink mixes are at the wrong end, and several liquor bottles are found knocked over. They say bottles will clink as if someone ran their hand over the tops of the bottles as they walked by. One day the shift manager was relaxing as she sat at the bar doing her paperwork. She glanced up to see a lady glide across the dance floor and disappear into the storage room. The restaurant was closed, so she grabbed another coworker; they checked the storeroom to find nobody in there.

Many times employees have seen the rocker in front of the fireplace slowly tilting as if someone was seated in the chair. A group of co-workers returned after closing to pick up a misplaced item. They saw the chair gently rocking in the dark near the hearth. The sight of the unoccupied moving chair scared them so much, they grabbed the forgotten item and ran out of the building as fast as they could.

Many guests come to the club and get photos and video with ghostlike images appearing in their photographs. They see fuzzy images of people in these photos but cannot make out the faces. I was in Flagstaff on business and asked some fellow coworkers to join me for dinner at the Museum Club. Not wanting to dine alone in their rooms or have another night of fast food, they took me up on the invitation. We found a table near the back bar area just incase the phantom lady bartender was on duty. We ordered our dinners and I wandered about the restaurant snapping pictures in all the known active areas.

"The fires have been lit in the hearth of the fireplace when no one is around," I announced to my friends, and snapped another photo. As the fireplace is a wood-burning device, hot embers cold easily re ignite the wood into a warm fire again. My friends immediately took two steps backwards just as a precaution.

A few orbs, most likely dust or reflection from the dance floor lights, were filmed that night, but no apparitions of a lady behind the bar or in the corner booth. A few EVP's were also recorded—a strong "hello" was heard on the digital recorder.

A Phoenix paranormal team, WCGAPS, investigated the Museum Club in February 2008. They set up several cameras and equipment throughout the building and were able to debunk several claims, including anomalies such as dust particles in the air and voices heard in the ladies' room, which they decided were most likely coming from the overhead storage room. They did capture several EVPs, including the deep voice of a male saying "Hello." The WCGAPS team believes the paranormal activity at the Museum Club is residual.

Another paranormal team, TAZPRS, did an overnight investigation and recorded many EVPs on their recording devices and filmed anomalies on both still and video cameras. You can explore their findings on youtube.com and the team web page.

Lights have been reported to flicker on and off. People passing by in their vehicles look over and notice the lights turning on and off after closing hours, too. With all the history of the Museum Club and the Mother Road it rests on, it is no wonder that the former roadhouse still holds the energy of its former owners and the drama played around it. Welcome to the Zoo!

The Museum Club
3404 E Route 66
Flagstaff, AZ 86004
928-526-9434
www.themuseumclub.com

Rod's Steak House, Williams

History

Rod's Steak House has been a top dining establishment in Williams, Arizona since it opened in August 1946. In its heyday it graced the famous Historic Route 66 and fed many a hungry traveler on the Mother Road. Located 60 miles south of the Grand Canyon, it has been visited by patrons of many foreign countries, United States and Arizona vacationers, and is a popular spot for locals in the area.

Rodney Graves moved to Arizona and bought a small café in Seligman, a neighboring town about 48 miles west of Williams. There he met his future wife, Helen, who was visiting family and friends. A short time later he sold the café and moved to Phoenix to be closer to Helen where she was a school teacher. Helen and Rod married in 1938 and together made a decision to move back up to northern Arizona. They selected the town of Williams as their new home. Rod bought the Grand Canyon Tavern, which he operated for almost seven years. The Graves decided a good steakhouse was needed in Williams. Rod sold his tavern, bought a piece of property, and began construction on a restaurant.

Rod's Steak House opened on August 23, 1946 at a prime location along Route 66. The registered trademark menu, die cut in the shape of a steer, is still in use at the restaurant today (with a few price changes, of course). Graves operated his steakhouse for twenty-one years until he retired in 1967. The restaurant has been managed by two additional owners—currently Lawrence and Stella Sanchez. During his teen years, Lawrence was employed at Rod's Steak House as a dishwasher and busboy and later as the manager. Today he still carries on the "Fine Rod's Tradition" that has made this restaurant a mainstay in Williams.

Ghosts

Some of the employees of Rod's Steak House say they have experienced the presence of ghosts or unexplained phenomena—perhaps ghostly travelers from old Route 66 are still stopping in for a bite to eat.

Employees believe the spirit of Rodney Graves is still managing his treasured restaurant from beyond. Near the entrance to Rod's old office (where he passed away just one day after he sold the restaurant in 1967) a large mirror once hung on the wall. Suddenly, it shattered from the inside out—as though someone pushed the mirror outward. Sometimes old photographs fall to the floor. The present owner lost one of his favorite rings. After weeks of searching every nook and cranny of the restaurant, he accepted the fact that his treasured piece of jewelry would never be found. A month later he discovered the ring sitting in clear view on top of the copy machine. Did the spirit of Graves place the piece of jewelry where it could be easily found?

The staff hears footsteps late at night when no patrons are in the building. A waiter reported he heard what sounded like boot steps on a tiled floor walking behind him. This might not seem unusual—but the floor in the restaurant is carpeted. One of the waitresses insisted that many of the employees feel a presence of someone in the downstairs hallway near the restrooms. She has also felt the presence of someone standing behind her as she worked. The young waitress was leaning high upon a ladder painting some trim work at the eatery when she felt someone bump her leg. She turned quickly, thinking it was a coworker pulling a prank, but nobody was there.

The owners and staff are convinced the ghost is just a protective spirit making sure the employees are safe and the visiting travelers are satisfied diners. Rod Graves is no doubt still looking over the old steakhouse—along with Domino, the large fiberglass statue of a steer who stands proudly near the front door.

Rod's Steak House
301 East Route 66
Williams, AZ 86046
928-635-2671
www.rods-steakhouse.com

Sultana Bar, Williams

History

Located in Williams, Arizona along old Route 66, the famous Sultana Bar claims to have the longest operating liquor license in the state of Arizona. The historic property sits proudly on the corner of Third Street. Grand Canyon Railway visitors stop in to mingle with the locals, enjoy a sandwich or burger, and belly up to the full bar service.

This 1912 concrete-block building once housed a saloon, billiard hall and silent movie theatre. During Prohibition years the Sultana Bar provided liquor and gambling for patrons by invitation only.

The Sultana was once the social center for the town of Williams and even housed a few of the city offices. Many City Hall meetings were organized and held in the saloon and theater. The first "talkie" movie show in Northern Arizona was premiered at the Sultana Theatre in 1930.

In the rear of the saloon, camouflaged by a janitor's broom closet, you will find a wooden trap door that leads down into a web of tunnels constructed by the Chinese rail workers as the railroad town developed back in 1882. During Prohibition years, these passageways were used for the running and storing of alcohol at a time when just mentioning the word was a crime. These dark tunnels were also rumored to have harbored outlaws on the run. They were even known to house dingy opium dens. The underground tunnels crisscrossed the downtown district beneath Fifth Street to First Street.

The saloon gained a bit of notoriety when Williams Deputy Sheriff, Victor H. Melick, suffered from two gunshot rounds and was killed in the alleyway behind the building between 3rd and 4th Streets off of Grant Avenue.

Ghosts

It's no surprise that the Sultana Bar is rumored to be haunted. Bartenders in the old saloon have seen and heard things in the establishment they cannot explain. One of the female bartenders recalled an eerie confrontation with a ghost on a Super Bowl Sunday. She was busy hanging banners and advertising signs on the walls when she felt someone touch her on the shoulder. She spun around, thinking it was one of the bar patrons, but nobody was near her. A short time later, one of the local Williams patrons playing pool had a similar experience.

Could former bootleggers still lurk in the labyrinthine maze of tunnels and unleash their spirits each time someone opens the wooden trapped door? Perhaps someday these portals will be sealed off for good and the old saloon will finally be at peace.

The Sultana Bar
301 W Route 66
Williams, AZ 86046
928-635-2021

Twisters, Williams

History

The building that houses the Twisters Soda Fountain was once a bustling Texaco Gas Station and motorist garage providing service on the highway passing through Williams, Arizona. Travelers along Route 66 stopped in to fill up at the full service station when it was common to have a service attendant fill your gas tank, check your oil, and clean your windows. When Williams and Route 66 were bypassed by Interstate 40 in the 1980's, the era of full service gas stations began a rapid decline as well. Eventually the building was deemed to be a perfect location for an old-fashioned 50's diner for today's vacationists to Williams and the Grand Canyon.

Twisters is a family owned and operated business in Williams, Arizona—the Gateway to the Grand Canyon. The décor is right out of the 50's malt shop era, down to the black and white tiled floors, red and white booths, and chrome tables and chairs. The diner features great Coca Cola drink flavors such as Vanilla, Cherry, Chocolate and more. Twisters offers ice cream treats such as old-fashioned ice cream sodas, banana splits, sundaes, and Route 66 Beer floats! Patrons will enjoy lunch or dinner in a café that features all of the 1950's favorites such as charbroiled burgers, hot dogs, fries, and onion rings. They were voted as one of the top 25 restaurants in Arizona by Arizona Highway Magazine in 2009.

Ghosts

Soon after the owners of Twisters completed their renovations of the 50's diner in 2008, they installed a state-of-the-art surveillance alarm system throughout the café that could be monitored from home if necessary. Nothing ever activated the motion sensor cameras—that is until one morning in October 2008 when an alert triggered the alarm at 3:01 A.M. Owner Jason Moore was astounded by what he observed on the surveillance recording.

What began as a white cloudy mist took on a shadowy human form and was seen walking in the storage/cooler area of the diner. The video recording was played over and over as Moore tried to come up with a logical explanation. This phenomenon has only occurred in the diner on that one occasion.

There have been a few other cases of paranormal activity noted within the Twisters diner as well. Items have fallen off of shelves for no reason. One of the owners was balancing the books in the early morning hours when she distinctly heard a man inside the building say, "Hello." Since she thought she was alone in the building, the voice immediately startled the female auditor. She decided to do a thorough search of the building. To her relief, not a living soul was found.

Several paranormal teams throughout Arizona have come to Williams to conduct investigations at Twisters. They set up night vision cameras in several locations of the diner in hopes of reenacting the phenomena captured on tape before. Some people speculate the ghost could be the former owner of the Texaco Gas Station from back in the 1950's. Clial T. Godwin, or 'Shorty' as he was known, was rumored to have committed suicide within the walls of the old service station.

Research by the MVD Ghostchasers team showed Godwin did commit suicide, but the grisly deed actually occurred west of Williams—about eighteen miles west of the town of Seligman. He carefully pulled his vehicle a few yards off of the busy Route 66 Highway. The distraught gas station owner ran a hose into the car from the exhaust pipe and put an end to his life. Could this perhaps be the reason the apparition in Twisters diner takes on the form of a misty vapor?

Stop at Twisters the next time you are visiting haunted Williams, Arizona. You are sure to enjoy good food, good music, and perhaps some full service care from its very own ghostly attendant.

Twisters
417 East Route 66
Williams, Arizona 86046
928-635-0266

Gila County

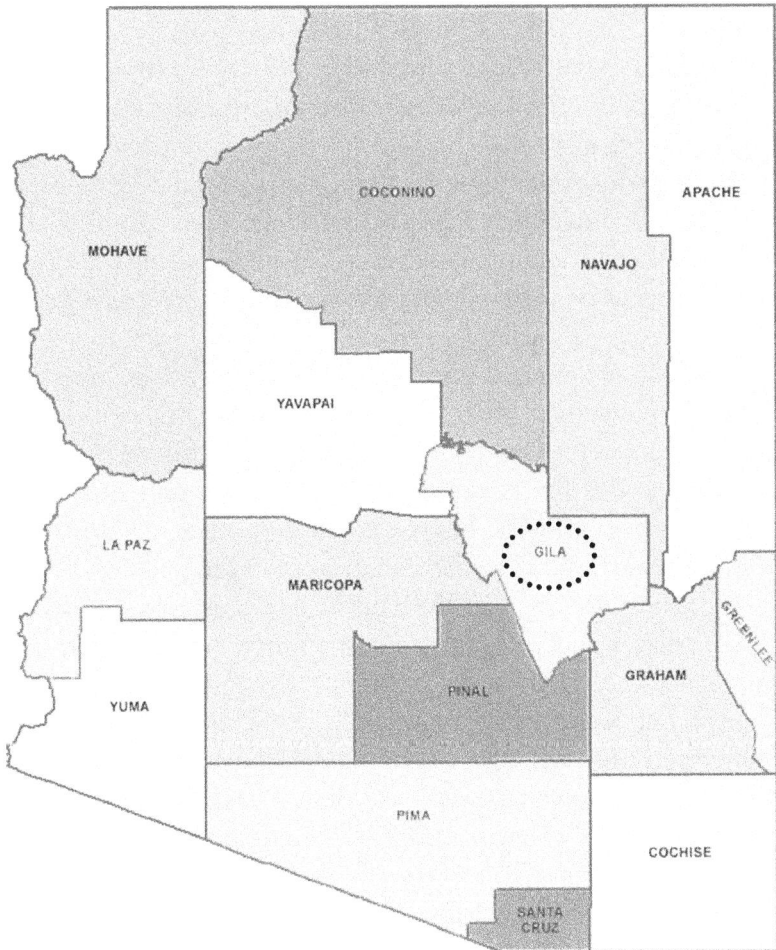

Drift Inn Saloon, Globe

History

Stephen, Dominic, and Alfred Rabogliatti sailed from Italy and settled in Globe, Arizona shortly after the turn of the 19th century. They began to live the American dream by constructing a 6000-square-foot building—the finest structure standing on Broad Street. The International House, as it was called, was constructed of adobe bricks by a local manufacturer. The upper façade was cast in decorative pressed metal around the windows and cornice, which proudly displayed the family name.

The bottom floor of the building was divided into three sections, or bays, with three entrances to separate businesses. The south end of the building was the Club House Café, the middle section was home to the notorious International Saloon, and the north end of the building had a business called Western Cash. There was also a sign near a stairway leading to the second story of the building. It read "International Rooms," and the stairs led to a prosperous brothel.

The madam had the largest room, at the top of the stairs. The ladies plied their trade in the twenty cribs that lined the hallways. This was one of the finest brothels in Globe. Prostitution remained a thriving business at the International House for several years. Eventually, the laws became more refined and the ladies of the night were forced to move elsewhere. The rooms became a legitimate boarding house for mining officials in town on business.

Downstairs, the International Saloon was wild and dangerous. Miners, cattlemen, and cowboys came from miles around to celebrate their successes and to belly up to the bar. They say there was a trough built in the center of the bar room floor so the male patrons could relieve themselves without making a trip to the outhouse. Loaded pistols were placed every few feet under the 30-foot-long bar for use by the bartenders in case things got out of hand. There were several gaming tables for faro and poker. A raised platform above the back door housed an armed guard who watched over the activities of the saloon.

Dominic and Alfred Rabogliatti raised their families in separate living quarters situated in the rear of the International House. Together the two brothers celebrated the joys and tragedies of their families with the backdrop of a bawdy bar room. Over the years the building has been occupied by several other businesses. It has housed a barber shop, restaurant, grocery store, furniture store and music store. The saloon has changed ownership several times as well. It has been known as the Owl Bar, Blackie's Tavern, and in 1980 it became the Drift Inn Saloon.

Globe is an easy day trip from Phoenix; so many people take a drive or ride their motorcycles up for the day and hang out at the Drift Inn Saloon after shopping in the antique stores and galleries. Guests feel as though they have stepped back in time when walking through the doors of the saloon. The Drift Inn Saloon has been restored to its former glory, from the wooden plank flooring to the punched tin ceilings. The building is now on the National Register of Historic Places, thanks to all of the work that has gone into the establishment since bartenders Lisa and Eileen took over the Drift Inn Saloon in 1997.

Ghosts

The owners of the Drift Inn Saloon greeted the MVD Ghostchasers outside of the building and related the story of how they came to purchase the old bar. They were passing through Globe on a road trip when they decided to stop and have a drink at the Drift Inn. They learned it was for sale and decided this was where their trail would end. They liked the small town quality of Globe and had a good feeling about the building—as though it had a special aura about it.

They opened a side door that led the MVD Ghostchasers to the second floor of the Rabogliatti building. This floor was once afloat with ladies of the night entertaining the gentlemen from down in the saloon and other prominent men of Globe who secretly climbed the forbidden stairs. They said the upstairs of the building is quite active with ghosts and not to be surprised to see or hear an occasional "unexplainable spirit of the past." Both men and ladies have been seen in the upstairs back hallway. A cowboy specter roams in silence as if searching for someone. The legend says that a jealous cowboy from Globe's early days came looking for his girl. He found her upstairs in one of the rooms of the International, where he maliciously shot and killed her.

Through research I learned the real reason behind the haunting of the old saloon and brothel. The tale was so chilling, it sounded as if it came from an old horror movie…and it is a part of Globe's greatest mysteries.

A young miner by the name of Joseph Ludwig was not known to be a ladies' man but was often seen in the company of certain women of the "tenderloin district." This 190-pound man was a gambler and lost most of his payroll earnings playing faro. Late in October 1907, he lost more than just another paycheck—this time he lost his heart.

Several of the working ladies of the tenderloin were hired at the International saloon as "bar rustlers." Male visitors to the saloon were often doped and then seduced upstairs to one of the rooms in the brothel. Once the door to the room was closed and the man lay passed out on the bed, the women would search the victim's coat and pants pockets for money, jewelry, and anything else of value. When the gentlemen came out of their stupor, often embarrassed or unsure of what had just occurred, they snuck out the back door and never told a soul where they had been.

It is assumed Joe Ludwig was hustled up to Room 18 by one of the ladies of the International Saloon. Whether the motive of his death was greed, self-defense, a twisted love affair, or a raging woman's revenge, will never be known. At some point in the night, Joe Ludwig's throat was ripped open with a blade and his heart was carved out of his chest. His body was carried out of the hotel and taken about a mile away to an unfrequented canyon, where it was blown up by giant powder in an attempt to destroy evidence of the crime. His body was found with a bloody towel wrapped around his neck, and his severed heart lay on the ground thirty feet away.

Bloodstained bedclothes and identification of the body showed that Ludwig's throat had been cut in Room 18 of the International Rooming House. It was also learned that he had suffered a minor stab wound a few days prior to the murder. Was one of the ladies working in the brothel possessively jealous and decided to put an end to his wandering eye? It has been noted that it was a custom of Southern Europe to cut out the heart of a man who has disrespected the family of another.

One year later, in November 1907, another tragedy happened upstairs in Room 18 at the International Hotel. Even though the second crime did not seem so puzzling, there was something so uncanny that it was traced to a possible connection between the two. If the musty walls of Room 18 could talk, two tales of vicious crimes would probably be told.

One Sunday afternoon, the body of Richard Veckland, a 25-year-old Finnish miner, was found in the bed in Room 18. The chambermaid discovered the remains about 2:00 in the afternoon and notified the authorities at once. Strangely, this was the same chambermaid who testified in the Ludwig case one year earlier. A post mortem examination showed Veckland came to his death by poisoning. The lungs were badly discolored and the heart clogged with blood turned black from the lungs. His stomach was sent to San Francisco for chemical analysis.

Saturday night, shortly before midnight, two police officers had come across a man standing in front of a house in the red light district. He appeared to be intoxicated to a point that he seemed like he had been drugged. He opened his eyes and the officers asked where he lived. In a weak voice he answered, "Room 18, International." The police officers escorted him to the hotel where he was taken and put to bed.

But what made Veckland say, "Room 18, International?" His friends indicated he did not have a room there. They reported he was rooming at the Central House on Broad Street—four blocks away. Was Veckland in some mysterious manner implicated in the Ludwig crime and in his drugged condition gave that answer because the effect of the drug brought back to his benumbed brain recollection of *that* crime?

When Veckland went to the tenderloin district with his companions, they said he had over $100 in his pockets. When he was picked up half-unconscious by the officers, he had not a cent on him.

The crime itself was easily explained. Veckland was undoubtedly given Chloral or "knockout dope" in his drink by some habitant of the brothel and robbed. There was probably no intent to cause his death, but he died from the effects of the drug.

I wondered about the housing that was in the rear of the old International. This was the place where one of the Rabogliatti brothers mourned the loss of nearly every one of his children due to pneumonia, car accidents, or death at childbirth. Were the spirits of these children still trapped in this building that once ran at full energy twenty four hours a day?

Back down in the saloon, the owners told us they have seen an old man or cowboy in a grey suit that stands behind the bar and sometimes drifts off into the kitchen and storage room. He often stands behind unsuspecting customers. He looks over their shoulders and never utters a word. When the surprised customer reaches out to the man, he simply disappears in thin air. Could he be one of the Rabogliatti brothers overseeing what is remaining of his American dream? Or is he a customer from the saloon's wild past stopping by to quench his thirst?

Bar stools are knocked over for no reason. Billiards chalk is seen flying through the air. You might catch movement out of the corner of your eye or feel an invisible touch on your shoulder. Personnel at the Drift Inn blame it on the ghosts. The bartender told us that a spirit from the past will occasionally call out his name. All these things happen when there are no patrons in the bar. The owners insist they are on good terms with the ghosts. Just don't be surprised to see or hear an occasional unexplainable spirit of the past…and "that ain't the liquor talking."

Drift Inn Saloon
636 N Broad St.
Globe, AZ 85501
928-425-9573
www.driftinnsaloon.com

La Casita Café, Globe

History

Considering that it is housed in a 135-year-old building, it is no wonder La Casita Café has a few ghosts housed within its walls. La Casita is situated on the south side of the former St. Elmo Hotel and was once a saloon and dance hall. The building had been divided in two sections over the years, allowing two separate businesses to prosper. The north side of the building housed a distinct saloon for a higher-class clientele. Both saloons shared a middle staircase accessible from a doorway off the street.

Late in the year of 1879, the few members of the Masonic fraternity residing at and in the vicinity of Globe, Arizona gathered to discuss the establishment of a lodge of Free & Accepted Masons. Mr. John Kennedy, an enterprising citizen of Globe and owner of St Elmo's, was persuaded to erect a second story onto the hotel. It was here the Masons gathered for their meeting place, with a five-year lease.

It is said that the notorious Big Nose Kate later leased the north side of the building in the 1880's and ran a brothel upstairs. The ladies' "hidey holes" for their money and valuables still remain cut in the floorboards of the upstairs rooms.

St. Elmo Hotel (later known as Club Verde) sat on the edge of Chinatown and directly in front of the famous hanging tree on Broad Street.

As Club Verde, the bar here was considered one of the wildest in the West (at least one murder occurred inside). Interestingly, there are still murals hidden behind the drywall of renovations of later years.

Salustia Rodrigues (Reynoso) came to Globe from Marfa, TX in 1926 with her mother after her father's death. Her mother owned and operated a cooking and cleaning service for the local miners. This is how Salustia met and married miner Pedro Reynoso.

Pedro and Salustia Reynoso opened the legendary La Casita Café in 1947. The La Casita Cafe soon flourished with the Reynoso's dream, adding their ingredients of hope, desire, and of course, Salustia's delicious recipes. Nana Salustia Reynoso's legendary Southwest dishes are still prepared today in the 3rd generations of La Casita Restaurants.

Ghosts

The staff at La Casita shared some of their ghost stories with MVD Ghostchasers Shiela McCurdy and Debe Branning one afternoon in October. The paranormal investigators had driven to Globe to attend *The Addams Family Musical* presented by the Cobre Valley Center of the Arts. They had a little time to spare and decided to stop in for a bite of Mexican food before attending the production.

"We have a ghost in the ladies' room," Annie, the manager, smiled as she refilled their glasses with more iced tea. "One of our patrons came flying out of the restroom claiming a man was standing inside the door. She was physically shaken."

"I've seen him too," claimed one of the waitresses. "When you go in there, be sure to stand near the toilet. Take your camera and aim for a photo on the inside of the doorway. That is where I saw him."

A paranormal team who has investigated the café in the past recorded a man's voice in the restroom that spoke using various medical terms. A loss of battery power was a constant issue during their late night investigation.

The men's room has its share of paranormal abnormalities, too. To reach the men's bathroom one must pass through a doorway and walk down a side hallway near the kitchen which leads to the small bathroom. Sounds simple, but for some reason, young boys sometimes get locked behind the doorway leading from the side hallway back to the dining room. There is no door latch or door jamb to hold the door closed. A gentle turn of the knob by an adult will release the bewildered lad behind the door.

Although the owners of La Casita feel confident the spirits in their establishment are friendly, they have had the property blessed by Catholic priests many times. The local padre has allegedly noted a negative feeling near the area of the men's bathroom.

According to previous occupants, the upstairs is supposedly occupied by the ghost of "Lady Rose," a madam of former times, and a cowboy who hangs around the hallway who is unaware he is dead.

The owner/manager said she would be more than happy to take Shiela and I upstairs to show us the old brothel rooms on the second floor. We followed her through the kitchen to the outside of the building. We carefully climbed up a rickety set of wooden stairs to the rooftop over the kitchen. We then had to jump three feet down through a doorway into the hallway of the old second floor. This area is currently used as storage for the café. There were remnants of old wallpaper, faux carpeting linoleum floors and an old claw bathtub.

We also spied the hallway leading to the doorway that divides the two sections of the building. Both upper floor rooms were once used as a hotel and brothel. Some of the café staff has felt unseen eyes watching them in the darkened hallway.

The owner recalled her "nana" telling a story about a paranormal encounter that took place in the early days of the La Casita Café. It was very late, the café was closed for the night, and the staff had finished cleaning and left for home. The family had gone upstairs to their living quarters and decided to call it a night. All was calm and quiet as the family started to wind down after a busy day. Suddenly they heard noises coming from downstairs. Furniture was being moved, glasses clinked, and voices were reveling as though a party was going on. They immediately ran downstairs to confront the intruders, only to find the dining room completely dark and empty of any guests. Perhaps for that one moment, the ghosts of St. Elmo stopped in for one last toast or celebration.

La Casita Café
470 N Broad St.
Globe, AZ 85501
928-425-5029

.

Journigan House aka Main Street Grill, Payson

History

The Journigan House is a landmark restaurant located on Main Street in Payson, Arizona. The grill provides a fine dining experience in a warm and inviting setting. Julian Journigan and his family built their home on Main Street in 1925. The portion of the building visible from the street was once the front section of the Journigan home. Journigan has been credited with switching the mail delivery service from a horse-drawn carriage to a Cadillac in 1923. He and his wife sold the house in 1930, and a son lived on the property for many years. Although Journigan traveled a bit and had a love for working cattle ranches and mining, he continued to own the house until he suffered a fatal heart attack at the Sunflower Store in April 1941.

When those owners moved down to Phoenix in 1953, a third couple purchased the house. A popular tale of lore states that the wife suddenly disappeared, followed by the husband filling their cistern a third of the way with concrete, hinting of a possible murder. The current owner has pointed out the mysterious block of concrete poured for no plausible reason in the water heater storage closet to many visiting paranormal investigators searching for answers.

Mel and Janice Laumb purchased the house in September 1993. They renovated the building to its present layout by adding the rear section of the restaurant and the patio. The Laumb's opened a quaint restaurant called the Heritage House. There was a small gift shop within the building as well. In 2000, it was converted to the Mogollon Grill at Heritage House. Later, the owners changed the restaurant's name to Mad Dawg's and Mel's. When the couple split up, Mel lived there alone for several years. He died in an upstairs bedroom in 1998. In recent years, it was called the Main Street Grille, and is currently under operation as The Journigan House.

On the outside, The Journigan House looks like a visit to Grandma's house or a country cottage, complete with a white picket fence. A landscaped walkway takes you up to a front porch entrance. Inside you will find wood floors and a river rock fireplace which adds to the country feeling the dining room emits. There is also a sports bar area where you can enjoy your favorite teams on the large plasma TV's. Outside is an incredibly giant patio just perfect for a wedding or family gathering. The Journigan House is located in the heart of the town center of Payson and situated at the gateway to Pine country.

Ghosts

Ghost hunters and paranormal investigators have found the The Journigan House an intriguing place to visit to pursue their quest for capturing a ghost on digital cameras or audio devices. The MVD Ghostchasers first visited the restaurant when it was operating under the name of Mad Dawg's and Mel's Bar and Eatery. I happened to catch a local newscast featuring the unique establishment and its owners. During the broadcast, the ghost stories were mentioned and I immediately turned up the volume. Soon my paranormal team loaded up the car with cameras and recording devices and headed to Payson to check it out ourselves.

The owners, Mad Dawg and Mel, were always friendly and willing to share the latest antics from their ghostly visitors. They joked about the drink item "hot chocolate" printing on the guests' sales tickets even though the customers had not ordered the item. They showed me the shelf in the kitchen where the bottles of A 1 Steak Sauce had been seen flying through the air. They had heard the sound of children's laughter. They told us about a steel fire door that opened and closed on its own. Appliances such as the coffee pot would be found plugged into the socket in the morning—even after they had verified everything was unplugged the night before. And of course, they had the traditional reports of the lights in the building flashing on and off during the night after closing.

A paranormal team from Missouri had heard the stories too. They decided to stop at Mad Dawg's and Mel's during their paranormal vacation road trip through Arizona in November 2004. During their conversations with the owners, their Trifield EMF Meter would spike every time "hot chocolate" was mentioned. Bar stools could be heard dragging across the floor while they were investigating other rooms in the restaurant. When they entered the rooms to check on the noise, they found a stool had been moved three feet from its original location. Near the bar, they witnessed hearing a faint conversation between a man and a woman chatting in another dimension.

Mel told us that many psychics report there is the ghost of an eight-year-old-girl in the building who died of an illness in 1914. Perhaps her family lived on the land where the Journigan house would later be built in 1925. Some of the employees have seen a child's pair of phantom footprints going across the floor. The psychics also reported an elderly man who died of an apparent heart attack seen in the upstairs apartment. Mr. Journigan did die of a heart attack at another location, but that might not stop him from visiting his former home. Out of the blue, one psychic told Mel that the spirit likes hot chocolate. It is unknown which one of the spirits trapped within the walls of 102 Main Street is the hot chocolate lover.

Arizona Paranormal Investigations, a team from the Phoenix area, did their own group investigation in November 2006 after the ownership of the restaurant had switched to Main Street Grille. While their goal is to prove and record haunted afterlife at locations, they are also determined to debunk anything that can be rationalized as non-paranormal. API Team Member James Kelly said they experienced several paranormal events during the night of their investigation of the Main Street Grille:

"A number of strange things happened to us that night. During our final EVP session, at 04:30, we were gathered in the bar area where there had been many reports of object movement and ghostly voices being heard by both patrons and employees of the business. There were nine of us gathered in a circle. Several audio recorders were situated around the perimeter of the circle. When we began to ask questions, almost at once we began to hear banging and thumping sounds in back of the bar."

The investigator beside me then asked, "How many of you are there?"

I heard a very loud, female voice respond with, "There are five!"

Startled with this, I noticed that the investigator to my direct right looked straight at me and said she heard the female voice state "There are four!"

When I found out that none of the other people in the circle heard this unidentified female voice, I was sure the EVP was captured on audio. It wasn't. I was stunned and perplexed. Whom, or what, had communicated with only us and not the others?"

Black Moon Paranormal, based in Payson, Arizona, had always known about the activity at the Journigan House. They had heard that Mel had passed away upstairs and that there were reports of sightings of a small girl. The team was very excited when the owner, Jimmy Johnson, gave them permission to do an after-hours investigation in 2013. They arrived on a Sunday night and proceeded to take pictures and decided to try a flashlight session to see if they could get any information that coincided with what they already knew about Mel and the young girl. Mel's spirit took a liking to their lead investigator Frank who asked Mel if he could have permission to photograph him. He was rewarded with several interesting photos including orbs and a blurred image. By going down the letters of the alphabet they learned the little girl's name was Iris. Iris had blonde hair and blue eyes. There is a picture of a young girl hanging in the dining room that is rumored to be her. She was about five years old when she passed away of tuberculosis.

Another paranormal team called Phoenix Scientific Paranormal Investigations stopped at Journigan House in 2013 to do their own ghostly research. They sat at a table using the twist top flashlight method for trying to communicate with the spirits by asking 'yes or no' questions. They asked the ghosts to turn off the flashlight if they were present in the room with them. The light flickered. The light faded. It lit back up bright. It went to black. Were they getting a response from the dearly departed tenants who had not left the house?

The manager reported to the team that he had seen the shadowy figure of a man in a cowboy hat casually leaning against the bar. As soon as he turned his head, the specter was gone! This could also explain the sound of heavy cowboy boots walking across the empty restaurant late at night.

The spirits at The Journigan House seem determined to stay, and given the friendly atmosphere inside, they fit right in. Oftentimes you can't tell the dead from the living on a busy evening—unless they vanish before paying for their order of hot chocolate they secretly added on to your bill.

Author's note: Journigan House closed in March 2015. The building is still standing and waiting for a new venue to take over the property.

The Journigan House
202 W Main St.
Payson, AZ 85541
928-472-6246

Maricopa County

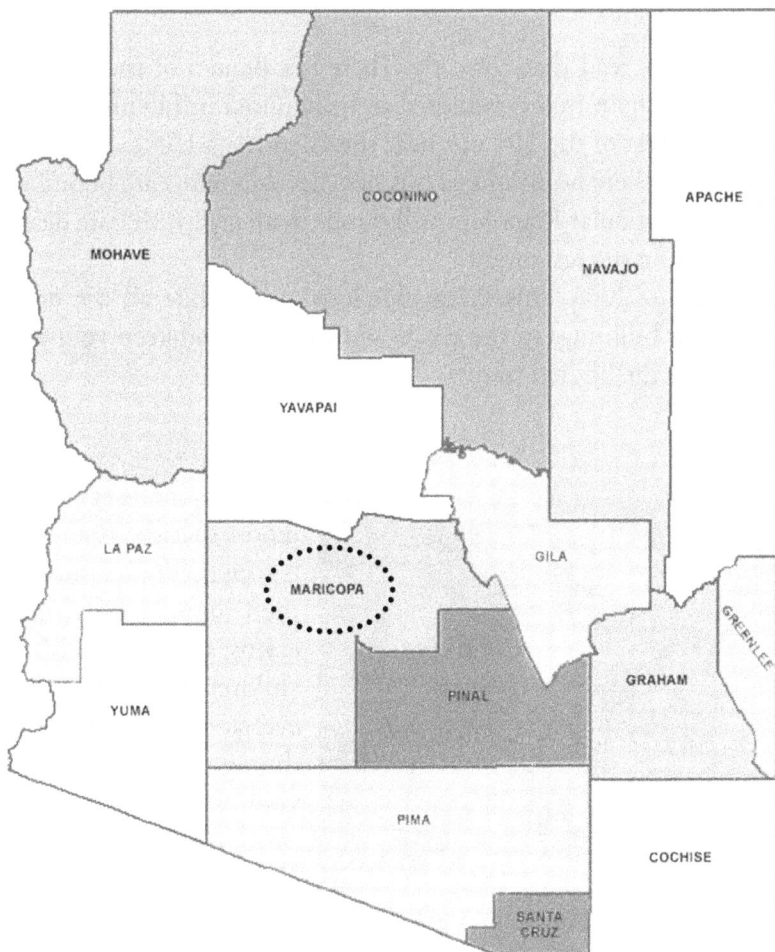

Pizza Hut, Glendale

History

Yes, you read that correctly. There is a branch of the national Pizza Hut chain that is rumored to be haunted in Litchfield Park, AZ. It is west of the 101 out near the Glendale athletic complexes in an area where housing and business developments are booming. But this particular Pizza Hut still stands in an area with bare desert surrounding the restaurant.

Built in 2001, this Pizza Hut looks much like all the other Pizza Hut buildings in the chain—just be sure and keep your eyes peeled for the big red roof.

Ghosts

Many internet sites report that the restaurant is supposedly haunted by the sounds of babies crying and the sounds of children talking whenever you are seated in the dining room enjoying your pepperoni pan pizza. Another one of the claims is that bathroom faucets in the facility turn on and off on their own.

Paranormal investigators with DarkHaunts. com explored the ghostly possibilities with a visit to the location in 2009. One of the first areas they checked was the restrooms. They wanted to see if the faucets were motion sensor driven. In the past this type of plumbing is known to give false on and off signals. Upon inspection it was noted there were no sensors—just a single handle on the faucet in the men's room. It was tough to manipulate as it was a bit calcified. They believed that if the faucets were turning on and off on their own accord that the spirits had to be putting a lot of effort behind the plumbing in order for them to move.

Palmer Miller recently contacted me with his own ghostly Pizza Hut tale. It seems his wife, Shauna, worked at the Glendale Pizza Hut for several years and was witness to her share of unexplained phenomena in the building. In or around the year 2007, it was closing time and the delivery driver had locked his keys in his car at his last delivery location, leaving Shauna with all of the closing duties in the restaurant.

Other than the fact that she was going to be burdened with a lot of extra tasks before she could lock up and go home, Shauna accepted her fate and began the closing duties. Suddenly she heard the water sprayer turn on and start blasting the kitchen. Then there was a loud crash. She dashed into the kitchen and saw that all of the pizza pan lids had fallen off the shelf. She shrugged her shoulders, picked them all up and went back to mopping up the front dining room. Then Shauna witnessed the most terrorizing moment of the entire evening. As she was mopping, Shauna happened to look up into the glass of the front door and there was a screaming woman's face standing behind her in the reflection! It was one shift she will always remember.

And keep in mind this particular Pizza Hut serves up both the best ghosts and "the best pizzas under one roof!"

Pizza Hut
13105 W Glendale Avenue
Litchfield Park, AZ 85340
623-935-5009

Inside the Bungalow, Mesa

History

If you are one of those who like a little spirit in your coffee, or a spot of supernatural in your tea, you just might enjoy a relaxing brew at Inside the Bungalow located in downtown Mesa's original town square. This was once the residence of a prominent Mesa doctor, Eli C. Openshaw. He and his growing family moved into the bungalow style home in the early 1910's. This turn-of-the-century house is tucked away behind beautiful flowers and plant life, and gives you the feeling of visiting your great aunt's home on a Sunday afternoon. The coffee house offers yoga classes, workshops, a romantic setting for a garden wedding, and one of the best locations where you might run into a ghost from the past. The mustard-colored bungalow with the unusual twisty-turvy brick chimney stands proudly on historic Robson Street.

Ghosts

Some say the pioneer spirits of the Openshaw family, residents from the early 1910's through the mid 1950's, still wander about their former home. Reports of ghost stories have surfaced ever since the house was converted into a coffee shop. Heavy paranormal activity was noted when a former business, Coffee Talk, operated in the building.

Many have seen a gentleman strolling from room to room or out in the back gardens of the bungalow. The owners told me of an incident where a customer was startled by the appearance of a woman in the ladies' room. Medora Openshaw is said to have died in the home in October 1957 of a heart ailment. She was 79 years old. Could this be the ghostly woman seen near the ladies restroom?

It has also been noted that the ghost of a young girl has been seen playing in the back yard as well. The Openshaws had several children in their home, and it was always open to many nieces and nephews who lived in the same Mesa neighborhood. One of the ghosts could be Openshaw's son, Noah G. Openshaw, who tragically drowned in the Salt River at the Roosevelt Dam during a family outing in March 1914. The ten-year-old stepped into the waters and was overcome by the whirling torrents of water. The funeral was held at the Openshaw home on Robson Street, and scores of people came by to pay their respects.

Owners Carrie Hensley and Betty Freeman confirm that the spirits at Inside the Bungalow are friendly and have caused no harm to any of their frequent patrons. They invite you to bring your friends and spend an evening on the patio where you can enjoy poetry, singing, or comedy three nights a week. It is also a great location for small meetings, weddings, light lunch, or board games. Their mission is to provide quality products and services, fun activities, and special events in a friendly historical setting...the ghostly spirits are simply viewed as that extra shot of cream in your coffee.

Inside the Bungalow
48 N. Robson St.
Mesa, AZ 85201
480-844-2353
www.insidethebungalow.com

The Landmark Restaurant, Mesa

History

The Landmark Restaurant's gabled roof building was once the home of a Mormon Church built back in 1908. The historic building is constructed of wood and red bricks and sits grandly along Main Street in Mesa, Arizona. On the east side of the church you will find Extension Road, where an open canal once flowed and nourished the large cottonwood trees that grew along its banks.

The church was housed in what is now the main dining room of the Landmark. The front door faced north to Main Street. The Sunday School rooms were downstairs. In 1939, the church underwent some extensive remodeling processes which updated the building to look much like it does today.

The two buildings south of the restaurant were added later and used for social events for the church. Both are constructed from adobe brick. The larger building is named Heritage Hall and was built for recreational purposes for the church in the late 1920's. This was a center for social events including plays and dances. People would come from miles around—even as far as Phoenix— to enjoy the dances and good times. The smaller building behind the patio was built in the 1930's for the Boy Scouts so they would have a proper meeting room.

By the 1950's, the congregation had multiplied and outgrown the facility. The church members moved to larger quarters in the Mesa area. An insurance company relocated their offices into the building and remained there for several years. Later, in 1963, the building became the original site of the Mesa Community College campus.

The first restaurant to occupy the building was open for business in 1972. Don and Candy Ellis moved to Arizona from the east coast and opened the Landmark Restaurant for business on New Year's Day 1981.

There are several banquet rooms available for special events such as luncheons, bridal showers, company dinners, rehearsal dinners or special get-togethers with friends or family. The upstairs dining room has an atmosphere that makes you want to wear your Sunday best for dinner, something rarely seen today. The Salad Room is renowned for providing a delicious and filling meal on its own.

Ghosts

The MVD Ghostchasers held their January 2005 Spirit Photography Workshop at the Landmark Restaurant. Team members Debe Branning, Nancy Heath, Maddie Kinder, Megan Taylor, Mark Christoph, Shiela McCurdy, and Chris McCurdy were joined by twenty-eight workshop attendees curious to learn more about the ghostly legends of the Landmark.

At 8:00 PM we gathered the group in the Garden Room, one of the spacious banquet rooms in the lower level of the restaurant. This was to be our base for the evening's investigation. The restaurant closed at 9:00 PM and the last of the patrons were departing through the front door by 9:30 PM. We now had access to the entire building as the staff quietly prepared the Landmark for the following day's business.

Everyone broke into small groups and began to investigate various rooms throughout the facility. Some went directly upstairs to photograph the Main Dining Room, the Clock Room and upper stairway. Others remained downstairs to check out the kitchen, the Victoria Room (which housed a mysterious closet under the staircase), and the bottom staircase where some feel a cool breeze passing them on the lower step.

And for some of the workshop crew, it meant dashing directly into the ladies' room where a woman's presence had been felt in the past and water faucets mysteriously turn on and off.

One of the staff members had keys to the large Heritage Hall and offered to let us in to further investigate the property. Almost everyone scurried off to the separate building to explore the hall and its basement. Many people photographed abnormalities on and around the stage. While almost everyone was filming in the Hall, we decided to send a couple of the many psychics participating in the workshop on a walk-through of the restaurant that was once the old church.

Tamara Jeffe began her walk upstairs with MVD Ghostchasers team member Maddie Kinder. Maddie jotted down Tamara's impressions as a crew member from AZCentral.com filmed the psychic at work. Tamara felt a strong, heavy energy in the dining room. The Mormon Church was originally housed in what is now the Main Dining Room. Later in photos, Chelby Geiss captured a moving orb close to the ground circulating between the chairs and table legs. The restaurant staff often feels off balance when they stand in the area near the wait staff work center in this dining room. Jeffe believed the room still carried deep emotions from its days as the Mormon Church.

James Kelly, a workshop group investigator who now is a paranormal investigator specializing in EVP, felt a sharp pain slice into his lower stomach area and almost doubled over as he entered the dining room. As he turned to exit, Tamara had entered the room and also remarked that something had passed through her and she, too felt a pain in her stomach. He found this to be an odd coincidence.

James also reported a major equipment failure in the Clock Room. Two ladies in the room were diligently using dowsing rods trying to locate spirit activity. As he scanned with a thermal temp device, the temperature in the room dropped from 69 degrees to 60 degrees within a second just as the rods twirled and popped. The temperature returned to 69 degrees as soon as the presence they detected was gone! As Tamara stepped into the Clock Room, she said she felt an angry male presence. She sensed many unresolved and emotional issues had remained behind in that room.

She did not sense extreme activity in the ladies' room. However, as the news crew cameras were filming, the battery packs suddenly lost power. Tamara then felt a cold chill and sensed weeping in the room.

In the downstairs Victoria Banquet Room, she felt a young girl lost in the cabinet closet under the staircase. She sensed the girl was afraid to go to the light. Tamara "saw" the number 15 and a name of Kristin or Ellen.

Meanwhile, team member Mark Christoph, who has done a lot of the MVD Ghostchasers video work, found himself a cozy spot in the basement of the Heritage Hall. It was there he chose to sit and communicate with the spirits in his own way. Mark sat alone in the dark basement for nearly thirty minutes. He filmed the depressing area with his night vision infrared camera. He said whatever was in the dank basement was beginning to affect him adversely. He suddenly became lightheaded, shaky, and sweaty even though it was a cold night.

Almost everyone who was brave enough to investigate the small dark basement felt a heavy presence and a sense of sadness, and not one of them wanted to stay down there very long. MVD Ghostchaser member Chris McCurdy is one of the first people on the team we like to send down to dark, dirty holes and creepy crawling places. Chris did not like the feeling he experienced in the tiny basement either and immediately came back upstairs.

Next, we sent out Yvonne Parkhill, another psychic who was attending the workshop, to explore the restaurant. This time MVD Ghostchaser Shiela McCurdy wrote down Yvonne's perceptions of the building as once again the camera crew followed closely behind.

Upstairs in the Main Dining Room, Yvonne's focus was on hearing the singing and music of praise that once filled the room. It also presented an underlying feeling of great sternness. The heavy feeling may have been residual energy brought on by the strict regimen of the Mormon religion of the time. She felt the presence of a man feared by all. He was almost godlike, perhaps the Bishop of the church, feared and revered by the congregation.

Nance Card came to participate in the evening workshop all the way from Nevada. In the Main Dining Room, she sensed a young girl's ears being "boxed" by her father, perhaps for not giving the religious service her undivided attention.

Yvonne felt a sanctuary in the Clock Room as though there was no public access and it was a quiet place used for reflections or meditation. Workshop attendee Lisa McDaniel felt a young woman looking out of a window of this room as though she was waiting for someone to return. This window once faced the original Main Street entrance of the church before it was changed to the current entrance on Extension Road, a side street.

The Salad Room is an entire room designated as a huge salad bar. Yvonne felt the hustle and bustle of female energy. Perhaps this was a ladies' meeting room at one time.

Back downstairs, we revisited the Victoria Room. Yvonne again felt the presence of a stern man of judgment. In the crawl space under the stairs, she sensed frightened children afraid of punishment. Lisa McDaniel also sensed a young child very scared in this dark closet.

This brought us back to the controversial ghost in the ladies' restroom. The restaurant staff has given the ghost the nickname of "Bea." Bea has been known to turn the sink faucets on and off. For a moment we all thought we had our own ghostly encounter with Bea. We were ending our walk-through with Yvonne and began to film once again in the restroom. Yvonne was "seeing" a dark-haired lady seeking solitude after being unfairly judged. As they photographed the restroom area waiting for Bea to show her presence, the faucets suddenly turned on and off, sending nearly everyone dashing out of the bathroom!

After we gathered our wits, we reviewed the video on the AZCentral.com camera. We hoped to see some phenomenal ghostly activity captured on the film. But, being a good ghost hunter means sometimes you have to be your own skeptic, too. Upon analyzing the video, we noticed someone had been photographing Yvonne with a digital camera and the flash triggered the infrared electronic eye sensors of the faucets.

Immediately, Debe Branning and Chris McCurdy set up a night vision infrared camera in the restroom to monitor any further activity. We also tested the faucets to try and debunk what had happened earlier. The flash from the digital camera triggered the electronic eye sensors as did any exaggerated arm waving movement near the faucets. Shiela McCurdy stated that she and another guest went back into the restroom and the faucets turned on without any camera flash. We have concluded that if Bea is lurking in the ladies' room, she is not in control of the plumbing.

Jason, a former busboy, learned I was doing research on the Landmark ghosts and contacted me with a story of his own. An older gentleman asked him for directions from the main dining room to the bathroom, which is located downstairs. A few minutes later, a crowd had gathered around the gentleman, as he had fallen down the second flight of stairs leading to the bathroom. He had crawled his way back up to the first flight of stairs in search of medical help. The man had been released from the hospital earlier that day after having extensive surgery. His fall caused internal bleeding and Jason watched the man die on the stairs as paramedics tried to save him.

About a month later, Jason was working his normal shift. A car accident in the area caused a power failure throughout parts of downtown Mesa, including the Landmark. The restaurant owner made the decision to stop serving and taking food orders. The employees were asked to box existing orders for the people that wanted to leave and escort them down the stairs to the front door. It was very hard to see down the stairway, so Jason was sent downstairs to grab as many candles as he could find in the lower party rooms and place them on the steps leading out of the restaurant. Eventually the restaurant was free of patrons and every employee worked as best they could to clean the dimly lit rooms of the Landmark. Jason was asked to return the candles downstairs and start cleaning and resetting tables in the Victoria Room. The Victoria Room is located directly to the right of the stairs and is the largest party room at the Landmark. If you stand in the room facing out, it's a straight shot down the 75-foot hallway leading to the Garden Room, the Bar Room and the Roosevelt Room. Each room is mentioned in order of distance from the Victoria Room, the Roosevelt Room being the farthest.

By the time Jason started cleaning the Victoria room, all the candles were placed back in their appropriate locations. It was still hard to see. While resetting one of the tables that sat directly to the inside left of the door, he noticed a gentleman walking down the long hallway. He was near the door to the Garden Room and walking away from Jason. He tried to address him by saying "Sir," but he failed to grab his attention. Again, in a bolder tone, Jason said "excuse me sir," but still no reaction. At this point he was thinking the gentleman was hard of hearing and was just trying to retrieve an article he left behind when the meal service was interrupted. He addressed him again loudly, "EXCUSE ME SIR, BUT THE RESTAURANT IS CLOSED AND YOU ARE NOT SUPPOSED TO BE DOWN HERE." The man said nothing and kept walking. Eventually the gentleman turned quickly into the Roosevelt Room. Jason stepped close behind him so he could escort him out of the restaurant safely. Jason made his way into the room to find absolutely no one in sight. The room was empty. He made one attempt to look under the tablecloth and then he ran out, back up the stairs and told his sister that he could no longer work there. That was his last day at the Landmark as an employee. As Jason looks back at this experience, he often wonders if this may had been the gentleman who fell down the stairs and passed away.

We took several group photos on the restaurant main staircase in hopes some of the ghostly patrons would pose with us. We noticed an orb sitting on Mark Christoph's shoulder in the photo. But he did not feel like anyone "attached" to him or followed him home from his episode in the basement.

Robin Abels, another workshop regular, sat on a bench at the foot of the lower stairs for quite a spell. She felt the energy of a small girl about eight years old in the area on the steps where guests and workers often feel a cold chill. Robin also photographed a swirling ectoplasm substance outside the main building late that night as she was leaving for home.

Several other paranormal teams have investigated the Landmark Restaurant as well. A local Phoenix Meet Up group arrived at the restaurant in 2007 and set up eight cameras in the Heritage Hall between the main level and basement area. They placed six more cameras in the various small and large dining rooms in the main building. The group broke up into smaller teams and rotated to each location in the large facility.

The team stationed in the basement of the Heritage Hall did not locate any EMF fluctuations. They conducted a few EVP sessions with no results. They placed a digital recorder in the crawl space and found a class C EVP that sounded like "help me." Although they found a few EMF spikes in the Main Dining Room and the Clock room, there was no audio or video evidence captured.

In 2007, another local team, WCGAPS, investigated the Landmark and were also able to debunk the bathroom faucet ghost due to the motion sensor devices installed in the ladies' room. They also determined that in the banquet rooms downstairs, the acoustics could easily pick up sounds and people talking from both inside and outside of the restaurant.

A paranormal team from Nevada, PROOF, arrived on the scene in 2013 to do their own investigation of the Landmark. One of their investigators saw a shadow walking by the French doors that led out into the courtyard. Another investigator saw the same thing just a few seconds before. They both went outside the doors to try and recreate the event but could not reconstruct what they had seen. The shadow moved very quickly and there was a small wall there. If someone alive had been walking by, they would have walked into the wall.

At the closing of PROOF's investigation, the Spirit Box repeatedly stated the word "dismissed" when the team asked if the spirits wanted them to leave.

The Landmark Restaurant is filled with spirits that share a strong emotional attachment to their former church. You will feel in awe when you sit down to dine in the elegant dining room. Leave a place setting across the table for an unseen guest and don't forget to say "Grace" before enjoying your meal. If you think you are hearing your name being called from the wait staff area, think again. It might not be questions about your meal.

Author's note: The Landmark Restaurant recently closed in May 2015. The building is being converted into a wedding venue where you will still be able to mingle with the spirits.

The Landmark Restaurant
809 W Main St.
Mesa, AZ 85201
480-962-4652

Queen's Pizzeria and Café, Mesa

History

In recent years, Queen's Pizzeria and Café has occupied the building at 12 W Main Street in Mesa, Arizona. The building was constructed of Lehi Brick. These adobe bricks were formed in the Lehi area from sand and cement. Straw was sometimes mixed with the cement to hold it together. Buildings on Main Street usually had a coat of stucco on the outside—and walls of brick on the inside to help keep the inhabitants cool.

The former location—directly next door at 125—has a history of former business within its walls. The area was once an enclosed breezeway. In 1911, it was listed as a meat or butcher shop as well as a sausage factory. The tiny shop doubled its size in 1923. The location opened as Apache Drug Company in June 1924 and was in operation until 1952, run by George N. Goodman, a former Mesa Mayor. George was president of the Arizona Pharmaceutical Association and his wife Clara became the first licensed female Pharmacist in Arizona.

The pizzeria has recently expanded and moved next door to a larger store location due to their successfully growing business. In 1911, this building was a grocery store with an oven in the back. This building decreased in size in 1923 as the meat shop next door expanded. In 1923, the address was listed as Dry Goods and Building Supplies. More additions were added in 1924, and at one time there were green glass tiles on the outer walls. Upton's Ice Cream Company and Upton's Malt Shop ran their business there in the 1940's, and later Mollie's Fashion and Fabrics offered goods for the ladies in 1952. At least three construction phases occurred in this building. The owners were wise in their planning. By adding additions only to the rear of the building, they avoided additional taxes!

Queen's Pizzeria is family owned and located in the heart of downtown Mesa. They take pride in creating fresh, delicious, made-to-order pizza, sandwiches, wings, calzones, and salads. They make and bake their own bread and pizza dough daily at Queen's. If you love dessert, they have brownies, cannoli, and Thrifty Ice Cream!

Ghosts

Queen's Pizzeria (the old location) has been featured on the Mesa Ghost Walk for several years in late October. One of the tour guides told the group the building is pretty active with paranormal activity. One day after a TV crew had been there doing an interview about the ghostly hauntings, an entire rack of pots and pans fell toppling over the counter. Almost all the employees say they have heard knocking on the beehive-style brick walls. The staff of Queen's Pizzeria & Café believes there is a prankster ghost who rearranges items in the kitchen and has the pans flying in air. They have also witnessed flickering lights, doors slamming, and heard the agonizing screams of a woman searching for her children. There are undocumented tales stating there was a fire in the old shop and a family perished in the flames. What looks like burn marks from a possible fire can still be seen on the upper part of the wall.

The new location of the pizzeria is filled with interesting ghost stories as well. Until 2012, the building was the site of Evermore Nevermore Clothing & Collectibles. The previous owner confessed he began to see unexplained phenomena starting with the day he toured the location with the landlord. During their tour they were surprised when the door to the women's restroom slowly opened on its own. The landlord took it in stride and simply reached over and pulled it closed again. On other occasions, the basement door has locked by itself and both restroom doors have been locked by unseen hands.

Their biggest surprise was when they discovered a hidden basement when a local electrician fell through floor while doing some rewiring at the store. Was this an old storage area? Or used for gambling and drinking during the Prohibition era?

One day a man in a gray coat was seen walking into the busy store—heading towards the back rooms. The owners realized they had not seen the man leave, so they began to search the entire store, but never did find him. Later that day, a paranormal group from Tucson did an investigation and lecture in the store. A sensitive woman with the group said she felt the presence of a man in a gray coat. That certainly caught the owners off guard!

The owner also mentioned that the CD player seemed manipulated. It switched from MP3 to CD and back again on its own and turned on and off whenever it had a whim to do so. He also noticed that there was a higher chance of activity on stormy days and had seen items fly off the shelves on their own.

Debe and Kenton of the MVD Ghostchasers met up with two members of the Ghosts of Arizona paranormal team to investigate the new location of the pizzeria shortly before renovations were to begin. Lindsey and his partner went down into the basement to do some EVP work while Debe and Kenton sat in the empty storefront hoping to observe a ghostly visitor. After forty-five minutes I began to "visualize" (in my mind's eye) men entering the doors of a business from another time, walking to a back room or perhaps the alleyway before one of the two additional building additions were in place, to engage in some "nonprofessional" activities. The investigation ended on a short note when Friday night revelers took over the outside walkways.

Stop by and grab some pizza and "spirits" the next time you are out on a Friday night cruising Main Street or attending one of the many City of Mesa events such as the art walk "Second Friday."

Queens Pizzeria & Café
127 W Main St.
Mesa, AZ 85201
480-964-1609
www.queenspizzeria.com

Woodshed II, Mesa

History

Nestled in a quiet strip mall shopping plaza, the Woodshed II stays almost hidden except to those patrons who frequent the busy sports bar regularly. Inside the bar and grill, autographed sports memorabilia covers the barnlike wood walls from floor to ceiling. There are several large screen TV's hanging from the ceiling so that you can catch your favorite sport from any direction you may wander in the restaurant. There are two pool tables in a room towards the back, and karaoke is offered on Saturday nights. A grill whips out hamburgers, fries and some of the best chicken fingers and wings in town.

The strip mall that houses the Woodshed II was built about 1985 on a lot that was vacant for a long time. One of the cross canals is close by and there has been evidence that the plaza might have been built on an Indian ruins site. I was invited to shadow another local ghost team called the Ghosts of Arizona Paranormal Society, led by Lindsay Brown, to an afterhours investigation of the Woodshed II.

Ghosts

The manager of the Woodshed, Rick, confessed that sometimes he sensed the former head bartender of the establishment, Gary, was still keeping tabs on the nightly business transactions. Gary was known to be quite the prankster bartender. He had a favorite place at the bar, under the TV that hung over the cash register area. During the course of a busy evening, Rick would lay paperwork in an orderly fashion at a spot above the register. When Rick returned to the restaurant after hours to catch up on his paperwork, he would find it scattered all over the floor. Rick decided it would be best to move the paperwork to the back office at shift's end in order to stop the ghostly prank from reoccurring.

The wait staff said most of the paranormal events happen after closing hours and mostly to the employees. One waitress told me she hated to wipe down the tables and chairs in the billiard room. It gave her an eerie feeling and she felt the need to get the job done fast and get the heck out of there.

Rick believes one of the most active spirits in the Woodshed is a deceased patron by the name of Ray. Ray was an elderly man who escaped the reality of his retirement world by spending eight hours each day at the Woodshed sipping on Jack Daniels and Coke. He had a special seat along the bar, the third stool from the end. It was here where Ray would sit and chat with several patrons who became his friends away from home. They say that after Ray died, certain people could feel his presence still sitting in his seat. Rick has noticed when patrons sit on Ray's coveted bar chair, they tend to drink a little more than usual.

"I was observing a woman drinking and sitting in Ray's chair," Rick stated, "As I was watching her, I noticed that she started to act kind of funny. First she started to talk to herself, and I really didn't think she had too much to drink at that point. Someone next to her was concerned and asked her if she was all right. She told the man that being a Native American she can sense things that other people can't. This made the concerned patron a little uneasy so he moved over to the next empty seat. As I kept watching her, I noted she was still talking to herself—or someone, and then she started to order Jack Daniels shots. This is when I knew something was wrong, because all she regularly ever drank was wine. I asked her to please move over a couple of seats so she would be away from Ray's chair. She moved over two chairs but continued to talk to someone in Ray's special seat. I asked her if she was sure she still wanted the shots. She told me she had a gift for "feeling things" that most folks don't, and no, she did not want the Jack Daniel shots anymore. She placed her hands on the bar and pushed back in her chair. She stood up and looked back at Ray's chair and told me she was not coming back to the Woodshed anymore. She told the chair "goodbye" and said something in her native tongue and walked out of the bar. No one else sat in the seat the rest of the night like there was something keeping them from occupying that particular chair."

A weekend bouncer was once joking around and playing "ghostly pranks" on some of the staff and the regular customers. He playfully tugged on their hair, lightly tapped them on the shoulder from behind, and pounded on the bathroom walls to frighten the ladies. Not believing a ghost was really present in the bar, he was making light of the situation by stirring up his own haunting with the occasional cry of "boo!" Just after last call, he started to perform his closing duties. He began to move and stack some of the extra chairs when "whack!" Something slammed the back of his head and knocked him into a chair, which caused an injury that would later require ten stitches. He immediately turned to defend himself and to look for whoever had hit him. Glancing upward, he noticed a speaker dangling from the ceiling—swinging slowly back and forth on its speaker wire. The speaker had been securely attached with a hook high in the wall and an eyelet on the speaker. The speaker would have had to been lifted up off the hook to come off the wall and fall on the bouncer's head. Many employees believe the ghost didn't take light of the bouncer's practical jokes and decided to play his own prank.

I experienced something paranormal in Ray's chair the evening of the investigation. I sat in the seat just to see what would happen if I "called in" Ray's spirit. After about ten minutes of meditation, I felt a burning sensation in my throat. It was that burning one feels when trying to learn to inhale a cigarette but swallowing the smoke instead. My voice became scratchy and hoarse. I asked Lindsay if he knew if Ray was a smoker. He told me that Ray did not smoke. But, Gary the bartender was indeed a heavy smoker and chain-smoked at the bar in the days before smoking was banned from drinking and eating establishments in the area. Do Ray's and Gary's spirits carry on by drinking and smoking through the souls of the living?

The Ghosts of Arizona Paranormal Society team continued their search for ghostly activity. They found the room with the billiard tables abounding with EMF spikes and at least a 10-degree temperature change. On a previous investigation they recorded what sounded like EVP messages in the pool room. One of the investigators thought he saw a dark shadow walk towards the kitchen area. Lindsay found that the recently charged batteries in all three of his cameras seemed to act as if they had suddenly become drained.

A large orb hovered in front of the picture that hangs over the bar of the deceased bartender, Gary. Gary was a loyal fifteen-year employee of the Woodshed, and most likely was keeping a watchful eye on the investigating crew.

A few days after the midnight-to-dawn investigation, Lindsay sent me an interesting photo. He had stopped at the Woodshed about 1pm for lunch. He took a picture of the outside of the building for the evidence file and captured a large orb in the daylight.

Some debunkers might say that the orb is just a reflection or sun flare, but here is the interesting part: Ray, the faithful patron and ghost, used to come to the bar every day at 1PM.

So, when you are at the Woodshed II enjoying burgers, wings or a pitcher of beer...beware of the seating arrangements at the bar. If you have a sudden urge for Jack Daniels and Coke, you better hope it is happy hour. You just might be drinking for two!

Woodshed II
430 N Dobson Rd. #13
Mesa, AZ 85201
480-844-7433

Lon's at the Hermosa Inn, Paradise Valley

History

Cowboy artist Alonzo "Lon" Megargee was a native of Philadelphia, Pennsylvania and ventured West in the early 1900's. He purchased six acres of land in what is now Paradise Valley in 1935. He built his studio of adobe bricks in the middle of the site and continued to build additions onto it. He called his home Los Arcos and later Casa Hermosa, meaning "beautiful house."

Megargee had no formal plans for the design of the building. He was influenced by architecture he had studied in Spain and Mexico. He chose to used old wooden beams from an abandoned mine and poured a mixture of oil and ash from the roof to give the impression of age to the exterior walls.

It is said the charming young artist was quite the ladies' man and wooed several wives and admirers over the years. He loved entertaining and hosting guests in his isolated retreat near Camelback Mountain. His guests enjoyed their serene and quiet visits to his adobe.

In its heyday, movie stars such as John Wayne and Clark Gable frequented the secluded hideaway. Due to the extended length of the stays of many of his guests, Megargee decided to run a guest ranch to supplement his artist's income.

Local law enforcement often suspected that Megargee used the ranch for illegal gambling, so he constructed a secret underground tunnel from the main building to the stables to provide an easy escape into the desert for himself and his guests should the law agencies make a surprise visit.

In 1941, Lon was in the middle of a divorce and needed money. He decided to put Casa Hermosa, complete with his art and furnishings, up for sale. Megargee later moved to Sedona, Arizona and passed away in the hospital in Cottonwood in January 1960 due to heart disease. He was 76 years old. Lon Megargee is buried in Greenwood Cemetery in Phoenix…but they say he still makes a visit to the Hermosa Inn from time to time.

The new owners planned to use the property as their private residence. One evening they were awkwardly surprised when old friends of Megargee arrived by taxi looking for a place to spend a quiet weekend. They suddenly found themselves in the guest ranch business, making Casa Hermosa into The Hermosa Inn. The new owners added a swimming pool, tennis courts, casitas, and villas.

In 1987, a terrible fire severely damaged the original building—Megargee's old home. The property was purchased by current owners Fred and Jennifer Unger in 1992. Following restoration of the adobe walls, charred beams, and ironwork in the main building, the property re-opened in 1994, again as the Hermosa Inn, now a 34-room luxury boutique resort, with a new restaurant, "Lon's at the Hermosa," named for Lon Megargee. The restaurant occupies the original building.

In 1995, the Hermosa Inn was featured in the movie *Waiting to Exhale*. Whitney Houston's character celebrates New Year's Eve in Lon's main dining room.

Ghosts

The Hermosa Inn is allegedly haunted by the ghost of its original owner, Alonzo Megargee. Guests and hotel staff have reported seeing the lanky cowboy in various locations throughout the inn. The friendly ghost of "Lon" often appears as a shadowy figure wearing his signature cowboy hat.

He is believed to be the culprit behind toilets flushing on their own, and his prankster spirit has been known to break glasses and bottles late at night. He has also tossed the menus stacked on the host stand up in the air and on to the floor.

A frequent guest entered the restaurant to show her visiting friends some of Lon Megargee's original artwork that is displayed in the Last Drop Bar. The bar is located in the portion of the Hermosa Inn that was Lon's actual art studio and residence. The host, who had his hands full of dining supplies, graciously showed them the way and walked into the other room. He returned moments later (still with an armload of supplies) and found one of the women looking up in the air.

The host, following her upward gaze, politely asked, "Is there something wrong? Is there a leak in the roof from our recent rains?"

"No," she looked puzzled and stroked the ends of her coifed hairstyle. "You just patted me on the head."

He motioned to his arms still full of napkins and dining accessories; he assured the guest he could not possibly have patted her head, as his hands were still full.

Strange things happen in the restaurant from time to time. Often the candlesticks will fall out of their candlestick holders, and other objects in the dining room seem to move on their own or get misplaced. Decorations on the host stand have been pushed off the pedestal by unseen hands, and while a host was talking to a guest at the bar, a bottle of tequila sailed off the shelf and broke several glasses. When these incidents happen the staff will lightheartedly joke, "Lon did it!" or "Oh, Lon must have done that."

Lon keeps his eye on the spirits in the cellar as well. Construction workers were doing some remodeling work in the underground wine cellar of Lon's. They often left various tools in disarray to go upstairs to get other work materials. When they returned to the cellar they would often find their work tools had been neatly placed all in a row.

There are several other spirits haunting the grounds in addition to Megargee. One of the restaurant's evening dishwashers refuses to work alone at night because she has seen children from days gone past still frolicking out in the parking lot late at night when she leaves, at 1 or 2AM in the morning. She has also seen the mysterious spirit they have nicknamed the "Pink Lady."

Many of the guests at the Hermosa Inn have asked, "Who is that lady in the pink gown walking over the bridge by the pool?" The mystery lady has been seen wearing a floor-length flowing pink gown of another era. She appears to guests late in the evening or early in the morning strolling across the wooden bridge near the swimming pool. The staff has no idea who the ghost might be. Could it be a 'guest' returning for yet another visit? Or could she be one of Lon's early wives or lady friends?

Apparently the spirit of Lon Megargee likes the doors of his former establishment closed. One of the housekeepers quit her job after having doors slam on their own multiple times while she was cleaning one of the most haunted guest casitas—Room 107. Another member of the housekeeping staff resigned due to witnessing the reflection of a cowboy that appeared in the mirror behind her—also in room 107. She quickly turned around only to find no one was there.

Recently, a reporter visiting from Germany asked guest services about the "night watchman" on the property. He told them he saw the "watchman" twice. Once he was spotted standing near the swimming pool, and once he was seen closing the doors to—you guessed it—Room 107. There is no night watchman employed at The Hermosa Inn and nobody was registered or staying in Room 107 during the German visitor's stay.

The friendly ghosts of The Hermosa Inn are quite active. Perhaps they are still stopping in for a weekend getaway to see their old friend Lon. Occasionally, during the month of October, the Hermosa Inn will offer Hermosa Hauntings special packages that include a Guided Ghost Tour of the property.

Lon's at The Hermosa Inn
5532 N Palo Cristi Rd.
Paradise Valley, AZ 85253
602-955-7878
www.Lons.com

Aunt Chilada's, Phoenix

History

The foundation of the building that houses the original section of Aunt Chilada's North Room was constructed in the 1890's as a supply depot and general store for local area miners working the Dreamy Drawl Mines.

The Dreamy Drawl earned its name due to the fact that mercury was in the air during the mining days, which put the men working the Rico Mercury Mine in sort of a "dreamy state of mind" after a long day's work.

Following the end of prohibition, Dave and Jesse Noble, the land owners at the time, applied for and were granted the first liquor license issued in the State of Arizona.

The manager and chef of the establishment noted that the owners of the old general store are "buried beneath the floor tiles of the place of business." This area of the restaurant is now a banquet room where guests come to dine and celebrate important occasions in their lives.

After the conversion of the general store into a restaurant and saloon, the eating place was first known as the Peek Steakhouse. Contrary to what it sounds like, the restaurant was not named the Peek because it was on some showy mountain top. It was actually one of Arizona's first "peek shows." The "peek" was up into the ceiling overlooking the bar area. Scantily dressed ladies would gingerly crawl though the attic and perform an exotic hootchie kootchie dance for the guests "peeking" up into a clear plexi-glass ceiling.

It was later renamed George's Ole in the 1960's. George Cocherham gathered together native stone and over 3,000 railroad ties from the area, and using the labor of some of his off-duty firefighter friends, he expanded the restaurant to its current size.

Bob Gosnell bought the restaurant in the 1980's and renamed it Aunt Chilada's. It was nicknamed "The Hideaway" by the locals. Ken Nagel came on board as overseer of food and beverage operations, and by 1995, Nagel and his family had become the dedicated owners of this fine establishment.

Ken Nagel states, "The lady (Aunt Chilada) with the past—has a bright future!"

Ghosts

Cindy Lee and Debe Branning arrived for lunch at Aunt Chilada's after a busy day of purchasing items for their latest cemetery fundraiser project. Of course, their real reason for stopping on that weekday afternoon was to gather a few ghost stories and perhaps encounter the resident ghosts.

Our guide for the afternoon was one of the four daughters of Ken Nagel. She has grown up working at the establishment in one form of the restaurant business or another.

"Come with me," she waved her hand—and of course we anxiously followed her into what is the oldest section of the restaurant—the banquet room. This particular dining area was where the original general store once stood. It is also the room where it is believed the first owners of the store are buried beneath the floorboards.

"This is the room where most of the guests and employees see the ghost," our guide told us. "There was a ghostly lady seen in the 1980's and she was dressed in Victorian style clothing, usually dressed in a white gown."

The employees noted that they have heard a lady whispering in the banquet room when no one is present. Sometimes they feel cold spots or have come into the room and witnessed the curtains blowing in the air when there was no possible wind draft. The lady in white stays in the banquet room and does no harm to the guests.

Doors they have secured and locked at the end of the night are sometimes found wide open. Lights have been known to mysteriously flicker on and off for no reason.

The other active paranormal spot is in the Cantina where the "peek" show once held the spotlight. Many times when the staff members come out of the liquor room they will hear a woman's laughter—as though they are being taunted by the ghost.

Oh, and while you are there, ask your waitress to let you have a peek at the plexi-glass "peek show" window. It is now situated as a window with views of the outdoors in one of the several dining areas. And perhaps you will be able to sneak a peek at the ghosts of Aunt Chilada's too!

Aunt Chilada's
7330 N Dreamy Draw Drive
Phoenix, AZ 85020
602-944-1286
www.auntchiladas.com

Café Tranquilo, Phoenix

History

Café Tranquilo is the place in which to dine when staying at the swanky Clarendon Hotel and Spa in Phoenix, or simply grab a drink or a bite to eat while in the neighborhood. The Clarendon offers boutique hotel amenities, pool and cabanas, gourmet southwestern food and Phoenix skyline views. It is a locally owned and operated boutique hotel and is generally regarded by locals as being the most down-to-earth, relaxing and enjoyable hotel in Phoenix. They are not the biggest, newest, or fanciest hotel in town, but they make up for it with their service, pool area, rooftop deck and of course, the award winning restaurant, Café Tranquilo.

But not all was so fabulous on the grounds of The Clarendon in its early years. It was the scene of one of Phoenix's most tragic mysteries of the 1970's. It all began on a hot morning on June 2, 1976. Don Bolles was an investigative reporter for the Arizona Republic. He received a phone call from a man named John Harvey Adamson, asking him to meet at the Clarendon Hotel to conduct an interview to learn more information on the organized mob in Arizona (who was suspected of running their operations and brothel of beautiful women from the hotel.) This caller promised some strong evidence.

A meeting was scheduled at the Clarendon Hotel with Adamson to discuss information on what had become Bolles' passion—to expose the "Arizona Mob."

Bolles entered the Clarendon Hotel in search of Adamson, but never found him. After waiting patiently for thirty minutes or so, the reporter gave up and headed back to his car parked in the hotel's south parking lot. When Don Bolles turned on the ignition key, six sticks of dynamite exploded underneath the driver's seat, leaving him mortally wounded. His last words before losing consciousness were "They finally got me, The Mafia Emprise. Find John Adamson." Bolles died eleven days after the explosion. Does his ghost still haunt the hotel?

The north side of the building, where Café Tranquilo is located, was one of the more active areas of the hotel during the time the mobsters ruled the premises. Do some of the secrets of this organized crime group still linger in the hallway?

Ghosts

The MVD Ghostchasers conducted their Retro Paranormal Workshop at the Clarendon Hotel on July 19, 2013. The evening began in the Café Tranquilo restaurant with almost all of the investigators dressing in 70's retro style clothing. Immediately after dinner the group moved to the Don Bolles Conference Room (near the dining area) where "Hip Historian" Marshall Shore discussed some of the mysteries of the Clarendon Hotel and presented a slide show of another Phoenix mystery—the story of the Winnie Ruth Judd Trunk Murders back in 1931.

The investigators took a short break, then regrouped in the Don Bolles Conference Room where they assembled their own Electric Charge Detectors to add to their ghost hunting equipment bags. This simple circuit will detect the invisible fields of voltage which surrounds all electrical objects, including ghosts. The ECD can detect one volt. When a spirit goes by the ECD, the circuit LED light will dim—detecting your ghost. It was a great new tool for investigators to use during their investigative work in the Clarendon Hotel and Café Tranquilo.

After a thorough investigation of the three most haunted rooms in the hotel, investigator Cindy Lee brought a small group of ghost hunters back to the area of the Café Tranquilo not far from the hotel lobby. It was in the wee hours of the morning, the restaurant and lounge had been cleaned and chairs and stools stacked onto the tables. There was little or no activity on the entire property.

Earlier, the Café Tranquillo staff had shared stories of strange things they had witnessed in the café such as seeing shadowy figures out of the corner of their eye. Pots and pans and cooking utensils have moved about the kitchen or fallen to the floor. They have heard unexplained footsteps in the long hallway just outside the kitchen entrance.

This is where the group of investigators decided to set up their ghostly watch. At one time this hallway was merely access to meeting rooms—and the area known for a bit of shady mob activity. Cindy and Betty sat down on the floor in the area near the kitchen. As they gazed down the hallway they both saw a shadowy figure start to walk towards them and then stop—retract—and disappear. This happened at least two or three times. They began to feel uneasy and moved even farther down and away from the end of the hallway.

"It was like someone wanted to come down the hallway, but we were in their way," Cindy stated. "It gave us both a sick feeling to the stomach."

Other members of this late night investigating crew noted seeing a shadowy form in the kitchen serving area—close to the restaurant seating. As the group of investigators diminished in the early morning hours, Cindy sat in a comfortable padded lounge sofa near the restaurant seating area, eating an Otter Pop. Suddenly she heard the sound of a bar stool moving across the floor.

Thinking one of the investigators had wandered somewhere they did not have access too, she stood up to look around. There in the middle of the room, not far from where she had been sitting, was one of the bar stools. It was as though some unseen presence wanted to get her attention. Was it the shadowy figure they had seen earlier in the dimly lit hallway?

On a curious note, each time the MVD Ghostchasers team members arrived at the Clarendon to organize arrangements for the workshop, they found the space where Don Bolles was parked on that fateful day to always be vacant. Was this out of respect? Or, was it because guests refused to park there? Or did the spirit of Don Bolles keep vehicles away from impending danger in that particular parking spot? Perhaps one should always request valet parking!

Café Tranquilo
The Clarendon Hotel
401 W Clarendon Avenue
Phoenix, AZ 85013
602-469-1730
www.goclarendon.com

George & Dragon English Pub & Restaurant, Phoenix

History

The George and Dragon Pub and Restaurant is one of those friendly neighborhood spots that will have you believing you are toasting the Queen in a genuine old English pub where a large selection of imported beers and lagers await you. In the adjoining dining room, you can sample British treats like Shepherd's Pie, Fish and Chips, and Bangers and Mash.

Street maps of London enhance the décor of the walls while British flags hang proudly from the oak ceiling beams. There are two separate areas for dining. You can enjoy your meal in the pub area and watch the latest soccer game on the telly. Or choose a more romantic table in the dining area in the next room. A flagstone fireplace in the dining room adds to the English inn flavor.

Before the George and Dragon crowd began filling the building with good cheer and laughter, it was part of the Shakey's Pizza Parlor chain. As you watched pizzas being tossed into the air, you could enjoy watching silent movies and singing along with banjo players. There is an undocumented story that concerns a murder in the pizza parlor. The story says the girlfriend of an unfaithful cook came into the kitchen and shot her partner with a .22 caliber pistol.

The George and Dragon owner, David Wimberley, let me in on another secret of the property's past: it may have been built on a sacred Indian Burial Ground.

The old Phoenix Indian School grounds once graced the nearby area. The institute was an off reservation boarding school for the Native Americans in Arizona. For many years, the students were not allowed to leave the school grounds except to attend church on Sunday. Sometimes students would sneak away from the campus to play in the cottonwoods or cornfields close by. In later years, they were given more free time and permitted to leave the facility to visit their families. Parents or relatives often gave students certain amulets, effigies, fetishes, or charms that had religious importance. They hid these treasures from school officials, sometimes in the fields and empty lots nearby. Perhaps some of these icons are still connected to the pub's property.

Ghosts

The George and Dragon English Pub and Restaurant was one of the first places the MVD Ghostchasers investigated when the team formed in 1994. Ghost stories involving the pub and restaurant had been circulating in the media for a long time.

The MVD Ghostchasers team met for dinner in the dining room. We were seated near the fireplace and excited about the great food as well as doing a mini-investigation of the establishment. We laughed and toasted our friendship. Our team not only works together professionally, but also has an enduring friendship bond as well.

During dinner we spoke to our waitress about the ghost stories we had heard through the years. She was very eager to talk about the ghosts and had experienced some of the paranormal activity herself.

"There have been many times when I have prepared the table settings only to turn around and find the plates and silverware stacked back in a pile in the middle of the table", she reported.

"Almost all of us have heard our names being called out," another waitress laughed, "We stop…look all over the room and see nobody else in sight."

David Wimberley confirmed that statement when we interviewed him. "It is a female voice saying "Hello David" or whoever the employee in the room may be."

"An intelligent haunting," I suggested, knowing the spirit was interacting with the staff.

Old surveillance camera footage has supplied the media with evidence of items moving in the kitchen and food being tossed about the pantry. A remarkable shot of a potato leaving the burlap potato bag, floating across the room, and landing on the floor was witnessed by many viewers on a local newscast several years ago.

Our waitress said the cameras also captured a "spirited" couple dining at a table along the wall after hours when no one else was in the building. The couple was there one moment and then suddenly faded away.

The women's bathroom in the restaurant has been known for its paranormal mysteries. What seems like a normal ladies' room when you enter leaves you second guessing when you walk back out of the door. You get a profound feeling of being watched as you stand at the sink washing your hands. Women often hear a female voice or humming from the stalls when they thought they were alone in the room.

There was a feeling of disorientation in the bathroom and one of the girls felt a bit queasy to her stomach. I thought I heard someone in the end stall. I wanted to take a few more pictures, so I stood patiently wanting for "whomever" to finish their business and leave the room. But when I glanced under the stall, I found nobody there.

Several paranormal teams in the Valley have done their own investigations of the George and Dragon Pub and have successfully recorded EVP in the bathroom. During one Halloween season, a local newscast played back an EVP voice which clearly announced "I'm here." The bathroom still rates as one of the most active areas in the restaurant.

The female entity likes to throw things from the storage shelves near the kitchen. Cups fly off the shelves of the area in the back and bottles of beer explode in the air.

"Most things happen when it is very late and it's quiet," our waitress told us.

Wimberley has learned to live with the female ghost in his employ. He was offered by an out of state paranormal group that specializes in warding off demons to have them banish his ghost from the restaurant. He turned down their offer.

"Our ghost is not demonic", he told me. "She is mischievous and playful. She likes to tug on your hair, poke you in the back, or grab your arm or shoulder. She likes getting your attention, but she means no harm."

Renowned medium Allison DuBois frequents the pub and confirmed to Wimberley there are many spirits creating the paranormal activity connected to the building.

Keith Jackson, a manager at the pub, filled me in on a ghostly encounter experienced by a beer distributor making his routine delivery. As the distributor was unloading his goods, he heard a woman's voice call out his name and the ghostly spirit gave him a playful push. He refused to make any future deliveries to the restaurant.

In August of 2008, the MVD Ghostchasers team made a return visit to the George and Dragon Pub. Debe Branning and Shiela Mc Curdy represented the MVD Ghostchaser team. We invited Sharon Day and her son Alex, Mike Marsh, an independent film producer studying the paranormal field, and James Kelley of the Arizona Paranormal Investigator team who specializes in EVP work. Keith and his girlfriend remained with the team after hours as neutral witnesses to the events that were about to transpire.

When the patrons and staff were finally out of the building, our crew went to work setting up video cameras in four different areas. We covered the back kitchen area, front bar, dining room and bar dining area with night vision cameras. James placed about twenty digital recording devices throughout the entire building, including the bathrooms.

Once the equipment was placed and activated, we all gathered at a long table in the main dining room about 3:00 AM so we could begin a controlled EVP session. A controlled EVP session works best when all parties involved in an investigation stay together in one spot in order to control walking, whispering, and other environment sounds.

As we sat down in our chairs, I looked up at the bar in the next room to see a short shadowy person—or what I thought was a person—poke their head over the bar counter to look at the group and then disappear. I took a quick head count and noted that all of the investigation team members were already seated at the table. Later, Keith's companion told us she thought she had seen the same shadow person.

We began some basic questioning and asked if there was anyone present, and if they were male or female. Suddenly we heard a noise coming from the bathroom that seemed to be responding to our questions. It sounded like a person tugging rapidly on a paper towel machine. We all looked at each other in disbelief. My first thought was perhaps a ceiling air ventilation fan had a bad bushing. Keith said the fans had been disconnected for years. We continued our questioning, and almost every time, the mysterious paper towel machine noise would feed us with its answer.

About 4:00 AM, Keith decided to ask a question of his own.

"Is the spirit who haunts the pub any relation to David Wimberley?" he asked boldly.

As if on cue, the computer terminal screens along the bar began to slowly light up—one by one.

"Who's behind the bar?" I asked. Now I knew the shadowy figure I had seen earlier was not a figment of my imagination.

The lights on the screens grew brighter and suddenly the computer registers began to spill out the server's register receipts for the evening…something that was previously done at closing time. Then, one by one, the computer screens turned themselves back off. The energy in the air had wound down to almost zero.

We decided to change locations and headed to the tables and chairs in the bar dining area. We began another EVP session, but this time everything remained calm. Our visit from the spirits had ended.

Keith began to turn on a few of the house lights, and then he called me to come over to one of the computer registers.

"Take a look at this!" He held up the register tape that was dangling down to the floor.

On the top of the tape it showed David Wimberley's name printed as a server. Mr. Wimberley was not even in Arizona that night. He was visiting family in England and had no access to the George and Dragon computer system. Was the spirit trying to give us a clue that indeed he or she was related to David Wimberley?

On Halloween 2008, we had the pleasure of presenting the George and Dragon Pub as one of the most haunted places in the Phoenix area. Both David Wimberley and Debe Branning were interviewed for a Channel 15 TV news broadcast in a discussion of the haunting of the pub. I smiled as we wandered through the restaurant and pub. Haunted or not, it still had that friendly, "everybody knows your name" feeling—including the ghost.

George and Dragon English Pub and Restaurant
4240 N Central Avenue
Phoenix, AZ 85012
602-241-0018
www.georgeanddragonpub.net

Los Dos Molinos, Phoenix

History

Los Dos Molinos sits quietly on a corner of South Central Avenue in Phoenix below Baseline Road. It was once the adobe hacienda style home of one of America's favorite western movie stars, Tom Mix.

It was built in early 1907, during the heyday of Mix's movie career when he owned several private ranch homes in the Western deserts. Tom Mix's life was cut short while driving US Highway 80 (now Arizona State Route 79) in his 1937 Cord 812 Phaeton between Tucson and Phoenix. About eighteen miles south of Florence, Mix met straight on with some construction barriers at a bridge that had washed away in a flash flood. He was not able to stop in time. The car swerved and rolled into a gully wash, trapping his body underneath. An aluminum suitcase flew forward and struck Mix's head, shattering his skull and breaking his neck. He died at the scene.

Later the small hacienda complex became the site of Loman's Mortuary and Funeral Home—a claim often debated by local residents who are unsure whether it is factual or urban legend.

The proprietor of Los Dos Molinos acquired the building in 1982—and has been tantalizing the taste buds of locals with their hot New Mexico cuisine. The restaurant acquired its name due to the fact they had two old chili grinders belonging to ancestors on display. The "Molinos" (grinders) were used by family members in St Johns and the family ranch in New Mexico. When they saw their Molinos they could not think of a more appropriate name than "Los Dos Molinos,"or "The Two Grinders."

Ghosts

The debate on whether Los Dos Molinos was a morgue is over and the results are in. Debe Branning and Shiela McCurdy drove out to the restaurant for lunch and gathered the facts from the owner's granddaughter.

"Yes, it was once the Loman's Funeral Home," she confirmed, "The room you are dining in was once the chapel where the dearly departed would have been laid out for viewing."

"Where was the embalming room?" Shiela asked as she finished the last few bites of her enchilada.

"Why, right across our little courtyard in the small cantina building," the hostess smiled. Instead of embalming fluids, the guests are now embalming themselves with various liquors.

The larger dining facility on the property was once the main entrance, offices, and sales room of the mortuary.

We asked some of the staff about possible ghostly encounters with former souls of the funeral parlor. One waiter spoke of a time he was working when the heavy front door to the restaurant open wide on its own and slowly closed. "Many times I get a feeling that there is someone watching me when I'm out in the courtyard near the fountain—or opening and locking the gates."

The kitchen help noted seeing shadowy figures darting about the food prep area from out of the corners of their eyes. Pots and pans have fallen off racks with no explanation.

The owner's granddaughter remembered one afternoon when she was alone in the restaurant going over some paperwork. "I looked up to see a large painting on the wall that hangs over the booths lift up and fall flat on the table. That's about the strangest thing I have witnessed here. Our "spirits" seem to be at peace most of the time."

Some people in the community fear eating at the restaurant due to the fact it housed a crematory. Many believe it is taboo. They say spirits of people still mourn for the dead and have never left the building—no matter how much plaster they applied to the outside to make it look more like the old adobe home.

The South Mountain Motor Vehicle Department office stands a block away from the restaurant—the site of Loman's former location. We took a short drive to the present Loman's Funeral Home at 7th Avenue and Dobbins. Shiela and I looked at each other and started to laugh. Behind the funeral home stands the "ghostly remains" of the old MVD Office.

Was it planned or merely consequential that these two institutions are doomed to be located near one another?

Los Dos Molinos
8646 S Central Avenue
Phoenix, AZ 85042
602-243-9113
www.losdosmolinosphoenix.com

MacAlpine's Restaurant
& Soda Fountain, Phoenix

History

This retro-style soda fountain opened in 1929 as part of Burch's Seventh Street Pharmacy back when almost all pharmacies sold drinks, ice cream novelties, and a sandwich or grilled items.

In the early 1930s it came under new ownership and converted to Morris Zimmerman Pharmacy. After Zimmerman left, it operated under the name of Morris Pharmacy. It was purchased by Fred (Mac) MacAlpine in 1938.

The brick building was adjacent to a Pay n Takit grocery store where customers now enter the soda fountain and shop for a variety of antiques. While 7th Street may have been a two-lane dusty trail at one time, it didn't halt the likes of Barry Goldwater and Frank Lloyd Wright from stopping in to wet their whistle on a frosty milkshake or have a quick lunch while conducting business in downtown Phoenix.

Some say Las Vegas icon, Wayne Newton, used to make frequent visits to MacAlpine's and loved to sing along with the popular tunes playing on the old jukebox.

The current proprietor, Monica Heizenrader, has owned the establishment since 2001. The shelves that line the walls are from the original pharmacy. The soda fountain is original to its era and still serves up great chocolate shakes. The booths, however, are not original to MacAlpine's. They were brought to Phoenix from a restaurant back east. Heizenrader replaced the original flooring with Jadeite green linoleum tiles to give it that 1920s period look.

The décor holds memories of everything from the 1920s to through the 1950s, but it is the 1950s decade that visitors love the most. The vintage store and ice cream shop is a popular venue for everyone's end-of-the-day shopping spree in the greater Phoenix area.

Ghosts

Although, owner Monica Heizenrader has never seen or encountered the ghosts at MacAlpine's herself, she acknowledges their presence and is happy to share the stories of spirits seen by customers and staff.

"They say there is a spirit of a man who sits on a stool behind the front cash register and keeps an eye on the money and protectively watches over me and the store," Monica smiled.

Heizenrader is confident the ghosts at the old soda fountain have good intentions and has never heard tell of any bad ones. A gentleman who worked there from 1946 until 1991 noted he heard ghosts walking around in the attic. One night Monica and her daughter were in the establishment working late, doing some baking and they decided to take a break. They sat down on the couch and it felt like someone came along and sat down right next to them.

One of her daughters had a small gathering at the soda shop on New Year's Eve. As the group sat talking in the booths and tables, they all heard the sound of glass crashing to the floor. Thinking one of the valuable antiques had fallen to the tiles, they did a quick check throughout the entire building and found everything in its place, as it should be.

A regular customer who is a bit intuitive claims she has seen a man sitting at one of the back tables. He then suddenly vanishes when discovered.

Megan Taylor, who has been a long time ghost hunting companion of mine, was in the soda shop enjoying one of the frosty delights when she noticed a woman dressed in period clothing had entered through the front door. A lot of ladies—and women's groups—love stepping out in 1940s and 1950s vintage clothing and enjoy a trip to the soda shop to show off their fine dresses and hats. Megan suspected this was just one of these women stopping by to add to the atmosphere of the fountain.

"This lady really fit the fashion of the day to a tee," Megan told me. "I watched her as she walked past the fountain, past the booths and headed to the back where the old pharmacy counter once stood—only she suddenly disappeared just as she was about to walk through a wall."

One of the clerks in the retro store and vintage clothing area told us of seeing a woman standing outside the store window on a Saturday afternoon dressed to the nines in 1950s attire. She stood there for quite some time—like she was waiting for someone. And then she slowly vanished into thin air.

MacAlpine's Soda Fountain
2302 N 7th St.
Phoenix, AZ 85006
602-262-5545
www.macalpines.com

Macayo's Mexican Kitchens, Phoenix

History

This fine Mexican food tradition began in 1946 when high school sweethearts Woody and Victoria Johnson decided to open their first restaurant. The couple named their first eatery "Woody's El Nido." The small café with just six tables was located at 200 W. McDowell Street in Phoenix. It blossomed into something big, and they eventually moved to their current site on Central Avenue in 1952. They made a commitment to use only quality ingredients and serve it up with a warm and friendly manner—a commitment the family has carried on for decades.

The Johnson family now owns thirteen Macayo's establishments in Arizona and operates two more restaurants in Las Vegas, Nevada. They are all still family-owned and locally operated. Today, Macayo's is managed by the Johnson's daughter Sharisse and their two sons, Gary and Stephen.

In 2009, President Barack Obama, his wife Michelle, and daughters Malia and Sasha made local headlines when they dined at Macayo's Mexican Kitchen on Central Avenue. The First Family was secretly whisked in through a private entrance and served in a private dining area upstairs.

As the owners of Macayo's say, "Every family has their secrets, ours just happens to be recipes!"

Ghosts

Macayo's has been one of the most popular Mexican food restaurants on Central Avenue for over sixty years. In its first year of operation (1952), it was visited by popular celebrities such as Liberace, Fleetwood Mac, Bill Cosby, Wilt Chamberlain, Jim Nabors, Alice Cooper, and Elvira! The staff is never blown away by who may walk through the door!

Recently, ghost hunter Megan Taylor and her friend Maria decided to stop at Macayo's for lunch after spending the morning shopping at a nearby metaphysical store looking for crystals, charms and other magical items.

They parked in the back parking lot and walked into the main entrance, where they were immediately greeted by one of the restaurant staff members. They were escorted to the main dining room and seated in a booth somewhat near the wait station.

"This is a perfect spot," Megan smiled as she and her friend began to study the menu and snack on a serving of chips and salsa.

Moments later Megan looked up from the menu and saw something or someone wearing white dash left to right from one corner of the room to the area of the wait station. And then it quickly faded from sight. Megan did a double-take and didn't see anyone in the room matching up to the blurred apparition she had just witnessed.

"Do you think this place could be haunted?" Maria dipped a tortilla chip into the salsa.

"It just may be!" Megan quietly whispered what she had just experienced to Maria.

When the waitress returned to take their order, Megan just had to ask every ghost hunter's favorite question, "By any chance, is Macayo's known to be haunted?"

"You saw him, didn't you?" Christine, a longtime employee of restaurant smiled.

"Well, I saw something," Megan nodded, "It zipped past us so quickly. I know I saw something white—maybe a white shirt?"

"Yes, that's our ghost! We like to think that it is the former owner," Christine winked, "Many of us has seen his shadowy spirit walk through the restaurant from time to time—and he is always wearing a white shirt. He loved this place so much and was very proud of its success. I think he just returns to make sure everything is running like it should be!"

"You are probably right," the diners agreed.

"And he lets us know if there is an item out of place or there is something we need to take care of. We have heard glasses being moved, and sometimes the lights will begin to flicker," she tapped her order pad with her pencil, "But we all know he means well. It's sort of nice having him visit us once in a while."

So grab a seat in a booth near the wait station and have a look around the dining room. Perhaps you will see something more than just the "ghost peppers" used in the delicious recipes at Macayo's Mexican Kitchen.

Macayo's Mexican Kitchen
4001 N Central Avenue
Phoenix, AZ 85012
602-264-6141
www.macayo.com

La Piñata aka Mary Coyle Ice Cream Parlor, Phoenix

Author's note: This location was recently purchased and redesigned into a Mexican food venue called "La Piñata." The restaurant owner and staff report there is a friendly spirit who moves things around in the dining room. Kitchen workers have seen shadows moving about the room at various times as they prepare the meals. Although there is no ice machine in sight, ice chips have been reportedly tossed about the kitchen and entrance hall by unseen hands.

History

Sometimes a ghost hunter just *knows* a place is haunted or has a feeling a few spirits pay a visit from time to time. Seated at a cute set of white ice cream parlor chairs and table, I began to look around the room. I was slowly working on a dish of chocolate ice cream, an early birthday treat from one of my ghost hunting buddies, Cindy Lee. I pulled out my little journal and wrote a few lines on the tattered pages.

It wasn't long ago that Mary Coyle's famous parlor really did escape from becoming a ghost. Just days before it was to shut down, a decision attributed to the slow business economy, a longtime Mary Coyle fan jumped in and purchased the franchise. Phoenix patrons were delighted, and so was the ghost of Mary Coyle!

Mary Coyle and her husband Walter originally opened five Mary Coyle Ice Cream Parlors back in Akron, Ohio in 1937. Later, in 1951, the Coyle's decided to move out west and sold four out of the five stores they owned. They opened up the Phoenix store at 15th Avenue and Thomas, across from Phoenix College, in 1951.

Mary Coyle moved to its present location over 15 years ago, when the Kellys, who were in-laws of the Coyle's, took over the business.

Mary Coyle "screams" oldschool ice cream parlor. There are pink and white walls, old booths, and ice cream parlor tables and chairs. The waitresses wear pink poodle skirts, white blouses with Peter Pan collars, and the music highlights the fabulous 1950's.

Ghosts

So we had to ask the waitresses: had anything unexplained or paranormal happened at the Mary Coyle Ice Cream Parlor? Without skipping a beat, the girls told us unusual things had started happening during recent renovations. Silverware and napkins flew off of the tables in the booths, pictures on the walls were in disarray, and kitchen items were misplaced or tossed about. One worker had to leave the building when a package of paper towels was tossed at her in the bathroom. Once Mary Coyle's portrait was hung back in place on the wall, things seemed to quiet down—although occasionally something out of the ordinary still comes into play. Perhaps Mary still keeps a watchful eye on her beloved ice cream parlor.

Need a tasty place to treat your sweetie on Valentine's Day or any special celebration? Mary Coyle Ice Cream Parlor is the place to get your two scoops of "boo!" Best selection on the menu for a ghost hunter? Try the "Suicide" of course! It's vanilla ice cream covered with caramel & marshmallow toppings, chocolate chip ice cream covered with hot fudge, & penuche nut ice cream covered with caramel, garnished with cashews, almonds, & pecans and topped with whipped cream & a cherry. Yum!

La Piñata aka Mary Coyle Ol' Fashion Ice Cream Parlor
5521 N. 7th Ave.
Phoenix, AZ 85013
602-279-1763
www.lapinatarestaurantaz.com

Nobuo at Teeter aka Teeter House, Phoenix

History

Advertised as "An Authentic Victorian Tea Room," the Bouvier-Teeter House is a Midwestern style red-brick bungalow and was built in Phoenix, AZ by Leon Bouvier in 1899. He used the home as what would have been called a boarding house or apartments in its day. Bouvier sold the house to Eliza Teeter in 1911. She continued to rent out the small three-bedroom home in boarding house fashion until she moved into the dwelling in 1919. Teeter raised her family in the home and she died in the back bedroom, which was the Garden Dining Room of the Teeter House, at 96 years of age. She is buried in Double Butte Cemetery in Tempe, AZ.

The Teeter House is part of Phoenix's Heritage Square and owned by the city of Phoenix. Teeter House is now known as Nobuo at Teeter House. It is a refined Asian-style teahouse by day and funky izakaya by night. Enjoy a setting of the early 1900's, wood floors, awash in earth tones. And there is always the possibility of a visit from spirits of the former residents.

Ghosts

Because she died in the back part of the home in July 1965, it has often been rumored that the ghost of Eliza Teeter is the likely spirit haunting the tea house. She owned the home for over 50 years and it was a big part of her life.

I invited my daughter Nikki to come to the former Teeter House Tea Room for my birthday a couple of years ago. We left the bustling noise and traffic of downtown Phoenix behind us as we entered through the heavy wooden doors of the tea house. We asked to be seated in the Garden Dining Room area. We were escorted across the creaky wooden floor, which only added to the ambience of the stately old home.

We were lucky enough to have a member of the wait staff that knew several ghost stories tied to the tea house. She told us of incidents of pictures flying off the walls, cold spots, and unexplained noises and odors in the old home.

A cook in the kitchen had heard her name called out when there were no other people in the building. She had seen a woman walk through the restaurant and disappear. Kitchen items have been moved to other areas or turned up missing. Teeter's ghost has even been suspected of hiding keys under the kitchen sink.

Patrons hear unoccupied toilets flushing in the restroom, although this could be old plumbing at fault. The bathroom door seems to lock on its own. Guests get up to use the facilities, yank on the door, and find that it seems to be locked. They go back to their table, keeping one eye on the door, but no one is ever seen leaving the bathroom. The guests go back to the door to try again, and the second time it will open with ease. This same incident happened on a recent visit to the tea house when investigator Megan went to use the facilities. Staff has witnessed a roll of paper towels spin around the holder and unwind onto the bathroom floor.

Always prepared for a mini paranormal investigation, I opened up my bag and pulled out a small EMF meter and my digital camera. No unusual EMF readings were found, although I did feel a gentle hand touch my left shoulder. I began to snap photographs of various areas of the room, hoping Eliza Teeter would appear on my camera screen.

After the new owners acquired the Teeter House, they began a complete renovation—updating the floors, rooms, kitchen and bar. Owner Nobuo was working late one evening and decided to sleep in the back room so he could get an early start on his projects in the morning. Sometime in the middle of the night, he was awakened from a sound sleep by a loud phone ringing throughout the house. He could only describe the ring as being a tone you would hear in the early 1900's. He search everywhere in the small tea house but could not find the source of the ringing. He packed up and headed for home and has never stayed overnight in the Teeter House again.

One of the dining guests said, "Teeter House is supposed to be haunted by Mrs. Teeter herself and I swear I heard the toilet flushing and I never saw anyone come out of the bathroom. The staff showed us some pictures that were taken inside the home in which you can see the creepiest, old lady ghost face peering back at you. It was taken in the Green Dining Room. It freaked me out, but my mom liked it."

Patrons don't seem to mind the ghostly history. Most come for the nostalgic atmosphere and delicious teas and luncheons. Others come for an opportunity to sip tea with spirits from another era, or to enjoy the ambience of dining in a quiet Japanese teahouse. And if you desire, you can read your future in the tea leaves in the bottom of your cup!

Nobuo at Teeter House
622 E Adams St.
Phoenix, AZ 85004
602-254-0600
www.nobuofukuda.com

Old Spaghetti Factory, Phoenix

History

The popular Old Spaghetti Factory restaurant consists of two former Phoenix residences merged into one large building. Both the Cole Mansion and the Baker House were built in the 1920's and stand on north Central Avenue in Phoenix. The Cole family bought the Baker House in the 1940's. They renovated and connected the homes by knocking down two outer walls and adding an additional building in the center. A furniture store operated in the space as its first commercial occupant. The Cole family wanted to tear down the Baker House and build a modern store on the site, but their customers preferred shopping for furniture in a cozy home setting.

The Coles sold the business and store to the Barrow Family, who continued on with the furniture store tradition. In the 1970's, a Phoenix businessman discovered the building and the Spaghetti Company Restaurant was opened. In 1996, the Spaghetti Company sold the property to the Old Spaghetti Factory.

Ghosts

A popular ghost story has surfaced over the years about two Phoenix police officers that had a paranormal experience while enjoying their dinner at the popular restaurant in the summer of 2003. I recently sat down and spoke with Officers Jim and Jay at the scene of the crime—the Old Spaghetti Factory. It all began on a Sunday evening, about 7:00PM. The two uniformed officers were seated at a table near the trolley car and had just ordered their meals. Their waitress had just finished describing the dinner specials when both men heard a woman release a long, bloodcurdling scream coming from what sounded like the basement area. Their waitress acted like this was an ongoing occurrence in the restaurant and the horrifying scream below did not seem to disturb her. Immediately, the two men forgot about dinner and asked the staff to show them where the door to the basement was located. The wait staff informed the men that the door was locked and no one was allowed to go down there. The officers asked for the night manager, and the door, secured by several locks, was slowly opened. The area beyond the door was so dark that the officers had to dash out to their vehicles and grab their flashlights. Officer Jim climbed up the rickety wooden steps to the second floor. Tripping over torn carpeting, wires, and pieces of broken wall plaster, he found nobody hiding. Then the men dashed down to the basement, not knowing what horror they might find. Again, there was no crime scene. Instead, they found old dining room chairs artistically stacked from the floor to the ceiling in the form of a pyramid in the center of the room. Officers Jim and Jay called for the manager to come downstairs to see their strange discovery. Instead of being surprised, the manager seemed to be a little angry. "Not again!" was his reaction to the chair pyramid. He proceeded to tell the officers it took him almost two hours to untangled the pile of chairs the last time they mysteriously ended up in this fashion. With no victim or clue to what dimension the woman's scream came from, the officers headed back upstairs to finish their meal. They never told anyone what really happened that evening in fear of being ridiculed by family, friends and co-workers. The men are retired from the police force now and wanted to tell their story— and set the paranormal world straight on what they witnessed that summer night.

And for those wondering about that famous statement by the police concerning the second floor, *'Don't ever let anybody up there! Ever!'*—Officer Jim laughed and noted that was only a safety warning about the old rickety staircase and wooden landing, probably a bit more intense than a ghostly encounter.

Several years ago, there was a rumor stating an older gentleman was sleeping by the fireplace in the Baker House when an intruder broke in and murdered him, bashing his skull as he slept. Another tale speaks of a woman who may have been shot and killed in the basement in the 1930's. Her assailant has never been revealed. A psychic sensed a mother and child still roaming the vacant upstairs floors, confused with the new design of their former home.

There have been many paranormal events reported by staff and guests of the Old Spaghetti Factory. Paranormal teams from across the United States have come to try and solve these mind boggling phenomena.

One night about 1:00 AM, a hostess was completing her routine of turning off each lamp in the lobby. As she turned to lock the front door, she heard her name whispered in her ear. She turned around and said "yes?" believing it was a coworker coming to tell her something, but there was no one in the lobby. A week later she had another experience. Once again she was closing the restaurant and began her ritual of turning off the lamps. The circuit breaker was situated on a wall near the restrooms. She had learned there was an option of turning off all the lights from that vantage point rather than doing each light switch by hand. She opened the panel and threw the switch. She looked to the right of her head and saw a white spirally object floating in the air. She gasped and the swirling form vanished instantly.

Another waitress reported a spirit that seemed to harass her when she was first hired at the restaurant. She was carrying a tray full of drinks when it felt like someone stepped behind her and knocked the tray out of her hand, spilling the contents to the floor. Thinking it was a co-worker playing a mean prank on her, she spun around to see nobody was in sight. She sat down in a booth and told the spirit she liked her job and wanted to stay employed and to please leave her alone. The spirit respected her spunk and never bothered her again.

Management has had trouble keeping a cleaning crew in the past. Sometimes the cleanup duties were covered by the bus boys. One employee said he would come back in the morning to find all the tables and chairs stacked in a corner. They have seen the lights in the building flickering on and off and heard their names being called over and over. The employees have also heard a woman's sobbing coming from the basement. Upon checking, they found nothing down there except some mysterious underground tunnels that creep under Central Avenue.

Members of the MVD Ghostchasers investigating team met at the Spaghetti Factory one summer evening. Once the team gathered in the lobby, we walked around the dining room trying to absorb the energies and feelings in the building. About 9:00 PM the team gathered the equipment and met with the news media team and psychic Gertie Miles. A Spaghetti Factory employee unlocked the door that secured the most haunted areas of the building. This door led to the basement *and* upstairs of the north house—the old Baker house.

Mark Christoph began to film as we slowly descended the steps to the unfinished basement. We stood at the bottom of the stairs trying to focus in the total darkness. Immediately Gertie sensed entities in every direction. Mark continued to film with infrared lens as we jotted down EMF and temperature readings. Gertie sensed a vortex or portal in one of the adjoining rooms and instructed Mark to film in that area. The best video came from the second room of the basement. A large orb, almost apparition like, came through the solid wall and swirled past us. "This portal," said Gertie, "is the door through which the spirits come and go at the Spaghetti Factory."

Next, we went to the upper floor. Upstairs were three rooms and a bathroom. These rooms were part of the original house, and were later converted into apartments. Nevertheless, the rooms were in total despair. There's no electricity in either the basement or the upstairs area, so flashlights were mandatory. While the downstairs dining rooms are elegant and furnished with wonderful antiques and décor, time has forgotten the upstairs of the Baker house, and perhaps that is why the ghosts are comfortable and choose to stay behind.

The media crew finished filming in the restaurant and left us to do further investigating. I decided to work upstairs with a camcorder and small recording devices. Mark returned to the basement and initially felt a bit uneasy in the darkness. Once he started to film, the intensity relaxed. He walked further into the darkened rooms to set up the camera and let it record.

Mark came back upstairs to join Debe, Kenton Moore and Nancy Heath to set up more cameras. We began to do some digital camera work. Nancy sat quietly near the stairs landing in an old chair we found in a room. She heard a young girl's faint voice say "Mommy, mommy, mommy." Other paranormal teams have heard this same cry for "mommy" and unexplained whispers. The sounds of faint music of the 1930's or 1940's era has also been heard upstairs.

The audio recording devices were successful in receiving some EVP messages. When reviewing the evidence Mark discovered a female voice left a comment on his audio recorder. We discussed the EVP and it sounded as though the ghost was not happy with me being upstairs, and wanted me to go home.

We packed up to leave about 11:30PM. We hoped we had enough evidence to share with the news media crew to add to their story. Just as Mark was shutting off the audio recorder, the female voice answered us by stating the evidence was "already there" and confirmed by recording her message on the EVP devices.

Everyone grabbed a bag of equipment and began to head down the stairs to the lobby of the restaurant. My leg was suddenly entangled with a wire cord that had been lying on the floor the entire evening. As I wrestled to free my foot from the wire, we laughed about me being so clumsy. Later, after reviewing our evidence, we can only assume the lady ghost was trying to show me who was *really* in charge of the investigation.

The Old Spaghetti Factory
1418 N Central Avenue
Phoenix, AZ 85004
602-257-0380
www.osf.com

Seamus McCaffrey's Irish Pub and Restaurant, Phoenix

History

Seamus McCaffrey's Irish Pub and Restaurant stands next door to the haunted seven- story San Carlos Hotel in Phoenix, Arizona. It actually sits beneath the hotel swimming pool that guests can reach from the fourth floor of the hotel. Seamus McCaffrey's business space connecting to the hotel dates back to 1928 when the San Carlos first opened its doors to the public.

The former owner of the Dubliner, Seamus McCaffrey, opened the pub in 1991. The authentic Irish pub has been serving residents and out of state visitors Guinness and Stout on tap for over twenty years. The décor and atmosphere of the neighborhood bar gives you a feeling you stepped into a bawdy pub in old Dublin. Part of the tin ceiling workings came from the now-demolished Fox Theatre that once entertained patrons in downtown Phoenix.

Ghosts

Customers have been describing spirits of the ghostly kind within the pub for several years. A regular phantom pub patron is seen peripherally at the bar, and always reported sitting on the same bar stool. The staff was cleaning up in the early morning hours after a big New Year's Eve celebration had come to an end. The chairs were stacked on the tables and the bar stools were turned upside down on top of the bar. As the weary crew began to sweep the floor, the ghost's bar stool bounced down off the bar and back to its usual spot.

The spirit of a tall distinguished-looking man has also been sighted as he descends down the back staircase. Staff and patrons say he disappears as soon as he reaches the bottom steps.

Beware of that beautiful woman sitting at the end of the bar. As men from the bar approach the fair lady to buy her a drink, the ghostly damsel turns away and vanishes into thin air. This phantom lady is always elegantly dressed in red. Witnesses say there seems to be a black cloudy area where her mouth should be. Could this be one of the ladies who died a fiery death in the 1940's at the adjoining San Carlos, stopping by Seamus McCaffrey's for a nightcap?

The quaint little pub shares the same basement space with the neighboring San Carlos Hotel. Down below is where they store the extra beer kegs, alcohol, and supplies for the bar. The pub's bouncer made a trip down to the basement to carry up a case of wine to accommodate a busy evening at the bar. He admitted hearing the chatter of the famous ghostly children who are said to frequent the cavernous basement of the haunted hotel next door.

The businesses are both built over the grounds that once housed Phoenix's first schoolhouse. The playground was laid out in the area where the Irish pub now sits. There is also an old well down in the basement. Legends state that the well was considered sacred by early Native Americans. Keep in mind that an open well is considered to be a conduit for paranormal activity.

Seamus McCaffrey's has become the headquarters for the annual St Patrick's Day Celebration in downtown Phoenix. The city closes down Monroe Street so the lucky Irish can eat and drink in the streets all day. The front sidewalk patio is the perfect spot for you to do a wee bit of people or ghost watching any night of the week.

Seamus McCaffrey's Irish Pub and Restaurant
18 West Monroe St.
Phoenix, AZ 85003
602-253-6081
www.seamusmccaffreys.com

The Stockyards Steakhouse, Phoenix

History

The Stockyards Restaurant in Phoenix, Arizona has been added to the City of Phoenix Historical Register for its role in Arizona's cattle industry and its Old West architectural style. Edward A. Tovrea opened his Phoenix packing house west of 48th Street and Van Buren in 1919. The Tovrea Land and Cattle Company had grown to nearly 40,000 head of cattle with 200 acres of cattle pens and was known as the world's largest feedlot. His son, Philip E. Tovrea, continued to run most of the empire after Edward died in 1932.

The location for Stockyards Steakhouse began in 1947 as a simple 35-seat coffee counter serving the cattlemen who came to do business with Tovrea there in the administration offices. A fire in 1953 destroyed that building. In 1954, a larger two story structure was built on the property which included a large restaurant and bar. Philip's wife, Helen G. Tovrea, was involved with decorating the new establishment. The back bar was modeled after one in an old saloon in Superior, Arizona. The "1889 Saloon" has carved mahogany woodwork, Arizona terrazzo floors and a shimmering crystal chandelier.

Helen commissioned artist Katherine Patton to create colorful hand-painted murals in the saloon and in the Rose Banquet Room during the 1950's. The painting of the lady in the red dress has sparked some speculation of who the ghost in the restaurant might be. Patton was known to draw herself and other acquaintances into her paintings. Some believe the lady in red was actually the likeness of Mrs. Tovrea. Some patrons and owners say the lady in red "comes alive" in the late hours.

Ghosts

The Stockyards building is also reported to be haunted. Proprietor Gary Lasko contacted the paranormal group "Ghosts of Arizona" to come after closing hours and investigate some of the paranormal activity occurring from time to time. Lights turn on and off, the chandelier shakes, and mysterious voices are heard in the building when the crew is locking up. The staff hears muffled voices and sees shadows out of the corners of their eyes. Some report seeing a face of a woman in the ladies' room mirror, while others state they have seen a lady in a red dress walk from the saloon out into the hallway.

The Ghosts of Arizona team set up night vision cameras and recording devices in the saloon, hallway, kitchen, restroom and dining areas and began their investigation. The team director, Lindsay Brown, invited me and fellow MVD Ghostchaser team member Kenton to sit in on the investigation as observers.

I sat down in the booth where famous politicians and western movie actors dined in privacy in a partially secluded area of the main dining room. I asked the spirits of John Wayne, Barry Goldwater, or my special friend and hero, Ben Johnson, to join me if they were in the building. The Ghosts of Arizona team entered the dining room to do an EVP session. At the conclusion of the EVP session I spoke aloud and said, "If John, Barry, or Ben is in the building with your friends; please give us some sort of a sign. Go ahead and ping one of the wine glasses on this table."

Of course, nothing happened, and the ghost investigating team moved on to their next hot spot in the building. I remained seated. I was determined to make contact with a spirit, so I began to put myself in a semi-conscious trance state. Suddenly I had a "flash" (picture) in my head of a brown leather saddle with Ben Johnson's signature inscribed on the side. I know his signature, as I have several autographed photos signed by him. Immediately I opened my eyes and thought in my head, "Ben?" A few seconds later I heard a muffled ding on one of the wine glasses on the table. A shadow quickly glided over a plate on my left. I pulled out my cell phone and checked the time. It was exactly 11:31 pm.

I was curious to see if anything was recorded on the digital device lying on the table, or if the camera with night vision picked up the phenomena. The director of the Ghosts of Arizona team later informed me that a slight ding was recorded at the table on his recorder. I smiled with satisfaction. I had a good working friendship with Ben Johnson when he frequented the MVD offices, and was now elated that this alliance has continued in his afterlife.

Along with an elite group of frequent phantom diners, the number one ghostly suspect haunting the remodeled restaurant is believed to be Della Tovrea. Della, the second wife of Edward A Tovrea, was the fair maiden who reigned over the beautiful Tovrea Castle across the street on Washington. This is the famous "wedding cake" building still visible from Loop 202 which sparks curiosity in many passersby. Della spent a great deal of time at the Stockyards Restaurant as well. Employees say they have seen the likeness of Della flit through the dining room and hallways from time to time.

As the paranormal team reviewed and evaluated many hours of audio and video footage, I reminded them that much of the on and off ghostly activity could be related to the fact that they are surrounded by paranormal energy conductors! The building is near the Southern Pacific Railroad tracks, the Salt River, the Grand Canal, and the new Valley Metro Light Rail—all there to enhance paranormal activity when the setting is right.

When you are in the mood for a mouth-watering steak, or maybe an evening in one of Phoenix's most nostalgic restaurants, why not saunter on in and have a seat in one of the original black leather booths under the branding iron light fixtures. You could be sharing the table with a true western ghost!

Stockyards Restaurant
5009 E Washington St.
Phoenix, AZ 85034
602-273-7378
www.stockyardssteakhouse.com

Casey Moore's Oyster House, Tempe

History

This Colonial Revival home with Victorian details was built in 1910 by William and Mary Moeur on the corner of 9th and Ash in Tempe. It is executed in brick and the house remains with most of its original detail and stylish features. The two-story house is a fine example of a transition from Victorian to a classic box-style home. It is small yet very comfortable inside. The most outstanding feature is the copper bell cast roof. This quaint Tempe neighborhood was keyed to family in that era, and several other members of the Moeur family lived nearby. Relatives lived down the street or just around the corner from each other. Cousins played together in one another's yards and visited the homes regularly.

William Moeur was a respected businessman in Tempe. His brother Dr Benjamin Moeur was the governor of Arizona in the 1930's. Both William and Mary Moeur eventually died in their Tempe home. William died on Christmas Day in 1929 near the fireplace which was located in the living room area downstairs. Mary died two decades later on July 10, 1948 in an upstairs bedroom.

In the years to follow, the home was rumored to have become a brothel for a short period of time. It did function as a boarding house for ASU college students and perhaps as a popular spot for a partying crowd to come by, hang out with friends, and end up spending the night. It has been rumored that in around 1966 a young girl staying at the house was brutally murdered. One story states that there was a quarrel in an upstairs bedroom. Some say she was strangled or stabbed with a knife. Although these rumors have never been proven true, could it have been kept a mystery by a secret pact?

In 1973, the boarding house was sold and converted into a restaurant and bar appropriately named "Ninth and Ash." It became Casey Moore's in 1986 under the ownership of Patty St. Vincent. Casey Moore's Oyster House has gained a reputation for being a pearl to this historic old town Tempe neighborhood.

Ghosts

The MVD Ghostchasers team was asked to do a series of investigations with the news reporting team at Arizona Central.com and our first scheduled investigative haunt was at Casey Moore's. We all met after dining hours in the upstairs area of the restaurant. Eight members of our investigating crew were on hand to set up cameras and recording devices to monitor and record our findings. The Arizona Central crew brought their reporters, camera crew and a psychic named Gertie to round out the investigative merger.

The MVD Ghostchaser crew entered the small private dining areas above the bar first. Immediately, we felt as if someone was anticipating our arrival. The air became thicker. The hair on Mark's arms stood up on end.

Gertie came into the house next not knowing the stories of the ghosts and hauntings. As she walked up the stairs to the upper dining rooms, she felt a strong presence of someone hiding. Later when we played back our recording devices, we heard an EVP recording of a woman's voice say "Hi!" as Gertie approached the upstairs rooms. Other paranormal teams who have investigated the site have clearly recorded her voice as well.

One of the camera crew members heard laughter in her ear and another felt her head being stroked in the upstairs hallway. We were ready for a busy evening!

There have been many ghost tales circulating about Casey Moore's through the years. One of the most repeated occurrences is that neighbors see a woman dancing, or witness a loving couple doing a series of ballroom dances in front of the upstairs window. Some see lights turn on upstairs on their own. Motion detectors go off on their own accord. One neighbor who walked his dog past the house on a regular basis stated he would often hear crashing noises coming from upstairs or see a woman glancing out of the window. Neighbors call the police, but when they search the building they find no intruder.

One of the MVD Ghostchasers, Gary Tone, was a former City of Tempe police officer. He remembers responding to a possible intruder call at Casey Moore's. They started a search on the ground floor and slowly made their way to the upstairs rooms. There are several small attic closets that could be used for hiding in the rooms. Gary, being the smallest officer, was elected to climb into the tiny crawl spaces with flashlight in hand in pursuit of the phantom burglar. Once again, Tempe's finest came up empty-handed.

Employees have reported a mischievous spirit that rearranges the furniture upstairs dining room. They have found chairs lined up in a row leading across the dining room. A large picture flew off the wall—the nail still in its place. Table settings are rearranged with napkins moved and the silverware fanned out on the tables. Staff finds tossed food and utensils on the floor. Food brought up on the dumb waiter has been flipped over or has gone missing completely. They have heard ghostly laughter filtering through the building. No matter how orderly the staff arranges the dishes and tables each evening, they will sometimes find them in disarray the next morning. They occasionally hear a distant giggle while something is creating a ruckus in the dining room.

The bartenders have reported disappearing liquor bottles, being tapped roughly on the shoulder, or have seen rows of glasses falling at the same time off a rack. They have heard their names being called out loud by an unseen voice, and have had their neckties yanked by unseen hands.

Bartenders closing down for the evening have seen a figure of a woman out of the corner of their eye going up the staircase toward the dining area. One man dashed up the stairs to warn the lady that it was closing time and she could not be up there. He looked around and saw her standing in the corner in the Blue Room where a closet once stood. He approached her and again gave her fair warning it was time to leave the building. She just stared into the darkness. He reached out to give her a hand and she vanished. All the hair on the back of his neck stood on end!

The owners of the establishment have also heard their names being called out. One of the owners keeps a collection of spirit photos taken by patrons and other ghost hunters and proudly displays them if asked. They have seen and heard children playing upstairs that aren't really there. Owners say you can see them faintly, as though transparent, and when you look again, they are gone.

Prior roomers from back in the boarding house days have returned to Casey Moore's for a drink and talk about the seeing the face of a stern-looking girl standing behind them in the bathroom mirror as they shaved. They refer to her as "Sara" the ghost. She is almost always described as having pale skin, piercing eyes, and long black hair.

Many have seen the ghost of a woman floating in a doorway upstairs. She has a blank stare on her face and suddenly fades away into the darkness. They have experienced an uneasy feeling that they were not alone, accompanied by a cold breeze.

A local paranormal team, Ghosts of Arizona, reported they had seen black shadows move from the Blue Room and go down the stairs while they sat in the office watching the former manager working on his computer. While upstairs, a team member has been scratched by the spirit of a black cat. One evening, all of the silverware had been neatly set on the dining tables awaiting the next day's business. They returned to the room later that same evening and found all the silverware in a pile on the floor.

The night we did our investigation, we waited patiently until the bar closed and the smoke from the cigarettes dissipated. The film crew had left a few hours prior, and now there were just three of the investigating crew taking some last photos, using night vision video cameras and digital cameras.

We set up in the Blue Room—the most haunted room of all. A lamp shut off on its own. We found it was set on a timer, but it was not set for the correct day or time it went dark. Still we could not claim this as real phenomena.

About 1:45 am, Debe and Liz felt like they were walking out of balance in the upstairs dining room. They were being pulled, as if magnetized, to the east end of the room. Mark stepped inside and immediately felt nauseated. There was a definite change of atmosphere in the room from earlier in the evening.

At 2:15 am, we reset the cameras to film in that room one more time. Mark filmed a small ball of light that jetted across the floor and towards a table where Liz was seated. Other lights danced near the chairs as we filmed. Liz noticed the overhanging edge of the tablecloth swish as if someone had walked and brushed against it.

As we packed up our cameras and equipment, we all began to smell a faint hint of lilac perfume.

So if you are in the mood for some delicious seafood and spirits, Casey Moore's is the place to dine. Bring some friends and ask for the Blue Room upstairs. Hang on to your napkins and silverware, and don't let the spirits spill your beer.

Casey Moore's Oyster House
850 S Ash Avenue
Tempe, AZ 85281
480-968-9935
www.caseymoores.com

Monti's La Casa Vieja, Tempe

History

Monti's La Casa Vieja is located at the north end of Mill Avenue, just a few blocks from Arizona State University. Near the banks of the Salt River, and now Tempe Towne Lake, Monti's offers a unique dining setting that occupies an old adobe hacienda—one of the city's original pioneer homes and the oldest continuously occupied structure in the Phoenix metropolitan area.

The hacienda was constructed in 1871 by Charles Trumbull Hayden, the man whose name graces the Hayden Library at Arizona State University. It served as the residence for the Hayden family, who nicknamed their home "La Casa Vieja." In Spanish this translates as "The Old House." It was the birthplace of Carl Hayden, one of the most important people in Arizona history, who served as a soldier and congressman.

By 1876, the Haydens had turned their residence into a hotel, blacksmith shop, post office and general store. Records show there may have been a restaurant in operation at the site as early as the 1890's. It was most likely for the comfort of travelers crossing the Salt River on the ferry, or for others using the flour mill. The Hayden daughters operated a restaurant at the location until the 1930's.

Several proprietors ran the restaurant and bar from the Great Depression era until 1954, when Leonard F. Monti Sr. purchased the property. Realizing the restaurant's historic heritage, he merely added his last name, dubbing the business as Monti's La Casa Vieja.

Monti researched the history of La Casa Vieja and was able to gather photographs, memorabilia and relics that are on display throughout the restaurant. Carl Hayden enjoyed making frequent visits to his childhood home and offered several anecdotes and stories about the historic building.

In 1984 the Hayden house was listed on the National Register of Historic Places. Although there have been alterations and additions to the original "casa," a visit to Monti's La Casa Vieja is like stepping into Arizona's pre-statehood days. The adobe structure includes an original latilla mud ceiling in the oldest section of the building.

Find yourself a quiet, cozy corner in one of the fourteen dining areas or five banquet rooms. Begin your meal with Monti's signature rosemary-scented Roman bread. And, keep your eyes and ears open for the image of the cowboy or distant laughter in the Fountain Room.

Ghosts

If there is any place in Tempe that should be haunted, it is definitely La Casa Vieja. Considering its history and the fact that there have been a few deaths in the restaurant over the years, it is no wonder the energies have remained behind, thus leaving a stubborn ghost or two reluctant to leave. Some employees feel the ghosts of Charles Trumbull Hayden and his son Senator Carl Hayden are still roaming the rooms of their old casa.

A cowboy specter has been seen in the Mural Room. The cowboy was stretched out relaxing on one of the long padded benches. The ghost was decked out in boots and a well-worn cowboy hat. He slowly faded away as an awestruck bus boy stood there observing the strange visitor to the building.

There has been activity noted in the Fountain Room, which was once part of an open courtyard when the Hayden sisters operated their restaurant and tearoom. It is believed that one of Charles Trumbull Hayden's granddaughters died at a tender age and was buried close to the fountain. Although her remains were moved to a cemetery, there have always been reports of hearing children's voices near the fountain. Does the little girl's spirit still come to play at La Casa Viega? The relaxing courtyard is now enclosed and is one of the larger dining rooms. By day, the large fountain at the end of the room offers the tranquility of the soothing, trickling sound of the water. But late at night, the cleaning crews have heard the sounds of laughter and happy children playing in the area of the water feature and refuse to enter and clean the room.

Staff members in the spacious restaurant say they hear footsteps and whistling, and have witnessed flickering lights and cabinets opening and closing. Strange noises are often heard after the patrons leave and they are preparing the dining rooms for the next day's guests. Some paranormal investigators have witnessed a full apparition of a woman walking through the rooms of the restaurant.

Several members of the MVD Ghostchasers paranormal team decided to go to Monti's for a Valentine's Day celebration. They arrived for a late evening dinner in hopes of staying a bit longer after closing for one of their famous impromptu investigations. It paid off! They spoke to the hostess when they arrived at the door, and she assured them it would be no problem as the staff is normally there very late.

Just for fun the group snapped several photos in the dining room while they enjoyed their romantic dinner and drinks. The atmosphere in the building began to change, and they were certain they had gained the energies' curiosity. While waiting for dessert, Shiela and Debe left the table under the pretense of using the restroom. Out in the hallway they chatted with several waitresses who showed them where they had seen unexplained shadows or felt a presence of someone stepping closely behind them as they worked.

"Makes the hair on my arms and neck stand up on end just thinking about it!" a young waitress said as she wrung her hands and rubbed her arms as though she felt the chill again.

The restaurant was nearly empty now. MVD Ghostchasers members asked if they could step into the notorious Fountain Room which was now vacant and quiet to see if they could record some EVP on to the tape recorder they carried in their equipment bag. The hostess escorted the six ghost hunters into the room and they each took a seat at a table near the fountain, which was decorated with a delightful little cherub.

"Is there anyone who would like to speak to us?" Debe asked.

She paused for a few minutes and listened to the sound of the trickling fountain. Shiela and Maddie snapped a few more photos. They sat in silence for nearly twenty minutes, hoping for an EVP response on the recorder while digesting their meals.

The patient hostess, anxious to go home, finally escorted the group to the front door. The staff was ready to lock up and finish up the evening's work. The team of ghost hunters walked out to the parking lot and played back the old-school tape recording they had just made inside of Monti's from the Fountain Room. They played back the question asked and listened closely to the grind of the tape recorder. Suddenly, they looked at each other at the same time. On the recording device they could hear a faint giggle as if it was coming from a child. They were almost positive there were no small children in the area that evening, but one can never be sure. Did the MVD Ghostchasers have an encounter with Ruth or Sallie Hayden?

Nevertheless, the group looked forward to the next company dinner party they were invited to Monti's La Casa Vieja, and they hoped the next time they would encounter the ghostly cowboy from the Hayden Ferry days.

Author's note: Sadly, Monti's La Casa Vieja officially closed on November 17, 2014. The building is still there, but not operating as a restaurant.

Monti's La Casa Vieja
100 S Mill Avenue
Tempe, AZ 85281

Rúla Búla, Tempe

The luck of the Irish was bestowed on the owners of Rúla Búla when they discovered the old Andre building located on Mill Avenue in Tempe, AZ. This Victorian style structure was built in 1888 for the saddle business owned by Robert G Andre. Unfortunately, the building was destroyed by fire in 1899. Andre rebuilt the two-story building on the same site and was back in business in 1900 with Mr. C. G. Jones. The Jones family owned the property from 1912-1977. This historic structure also housed the Price Wickliffe's Furniture & Undertaker business from 1912-1929. It was also home to a newspaper, AZ Cotton Growers Association, US Post Office and a Masonic Lodge. The second floor was used as a boarding house and apartments.

Robert G Andre was born in France in 1847 and raised and educated in Germany. He came to the United States in the early 1870s and made harnesses and saddles for the troops stationed at Fort Grant. He later moved to Phoenix and then to Tempe where he opened his business on Mill Avenue. Andre left for a trip to the eastern part of Arizona and was expected to be gone for several weeks. He caught a ride on the local stagecoach and was in an accident near the Highland Canal just east of Mesa. He had been lying on top of the load when the stage struck a small chuck hole in the roadway. He fell and one wheel passed over his body, severely crushing his right shoulder. He later died from these injuries. Could Andre be the ghost that haunts the Rúla Búla Pub?

Rúla Búla was taken from the Irish Gaelic language. "Rí rá agus ruaille buaille" translates to "uproar and commotion," and this means you will find a celebration and good fortune each time you visit the pub! The décor of Rúla Búla pays a tribute to Mr. Andre with a saddle style saloon. In Ireland, a merchant's shop would often double as a neighborhood pub as well.

Ghosts

The staff at Rúla Búla often remarks about being watched by unseen eyes as they work. The wait staff says they occasionally feel someone standing behind them, yet when they turn around nobody is there. One of the bartenders has had experiences with the mysterious entities on more than one occasion. It usually happens in the same area at one corner of the bar. One evening, at about 11:00 PM, the bartender and an old looking guest were the only people sitting at the bar. The patron had ordered a drink and they struck up a conversation. The bartender turned his back for just a short moment to put away some glasses, and when he spun back around, the mysterious customer had vanished, leaving the full drink behind.

Late another night, the bartender began a discussion with an odd sort of customer who asked about the fires that had taken place in the Andre building. Besides the fire of 1899, a second fire— one hundred years later in 1999—almost destroyed the building as renovations for Rúla Búla began. Just as the customer stated that he believed nobody was injured in the fires, a glass popped up two feet in the air, dropped to the floor and shattered. Is the ghost of Rúla Búla Bula someone who died in the earlier fire?

Pull up a bar stool at the corner of the bar and maybe you'll will encounter a spirit or two. Whether it is the ghost of R. J. Andre, a fire victim, residue left behind from the undertaking business or energy from the many antiques that decorated the pub, you will feel a touch of Ireland right here in Arizona. They say a true Irish pub is distinguished by its "craic," an Irish term referring to positive interaction among people through conversation, stories and music. You will find this and more at Rula Bula.

Rúla Búla
401 S. Mill Avenue
Tempe, AZ 85281
480-929-9500
www.rulabula.com

Gold Nugget Restaurant, Wickenburg

History

The main structure of the building was first constructed in 1863. In 1890, Murphy's Grocery and the Wickenburg Post Office were added to the west, and a livery stable to the east. Expansion at the turn of the century again grew the structure.

During the late 1930's, the Post Office was moved to a new location and that space was converted into a saloon. Later in 1952, the back portion of the restaurant was added, expanding the establishment to nearly 8000 square feet, which included a three-tier dining room, an alcove, a foyer and a conference room.

The sparkling chandeliers in the main dining room are rare antiques that were imported from France. Some of the fixtures from the original café are still in use today.

A fire nearly destroyed the addition. The building was remodeled in 1980, at which time "The Rose" stained glass window and elaborate oak woodwork were added, along with the baby grand piano.

During another construction phase in the fall of 2006, workmen revealed an old sign that hung in the nearby Santa Fe Café. They say the cafe was never as big as the Gold Nugget, but it had good food—along with a bus stop.

Many famous personalities have dined at the historic Gold Nugget Restaurant, such as John Wayne, Clark Cable, Clint Eastwood, Nick Adams, Ben Johnson, Dan Quayle, Alice Cooper, Val Kilmer and Rex Maughan. In recent years, the Gold Nugget has served famous fashion designer Mark Jacobs, supermodel Kate Moss, Former Alaska Senator Red Stevens, and Brent Strom, the St. Louis Cardinals' pitching coach.

Ghosts

Many strange sightings and occurrences have the employees and patrons claiming the historic building holds a ghost in residence.

Rumors state that the ghost is the spirit of a man shot and killed by his lover's husband in a jealous rage.

Tour guide/historian "Madam Mariah" told her guests about the Ghost of the Rose Room. It seems that a cowboy came to Wickenburg looking for a bride to share his homestead. Avoiding the ladies of the night in the brothels across the street, the young man frequented the café and was impressed by the lovely waitresses working there. He became infatuated with a lovely waitress working in what is now the Rose Room. This particular young lady had a smooth way of talking and could make anything on the menu sound mouthwateringly delicious. Soon the cowboy was madly in love with the waitress and purchased the finest diamond ring he could find in Phoenix. One evening the cowboy arrived at the restaurant, ready to make his bold marriage proposal. The beautiful young waitress was taken back as the cowboy asked her to be his wife on bended knee. After all, she treated each and every one of her frequent customers with the same flamboyant style—anything to sell another piece of pie and earn that coveted tip.

Apparently, the woman's husband, who was sitting up in the upper balcony of the restaurant, didn't welcome the marriage offer either. He shot the amorous cowboy on the spot.

They say the ghost of the cowboy is still in the Rose Room and plays with the light fixtures and moves the chandeliers. Occasionally, the player piano will play a melody on its own—slow and sweet, a bit off key, but nobody said the ghost was a good piano player.

A restaurant employee named Lillian has seen a ghost in the Gold Nugget Restaurant. The restaurant host/waitress encountered the ghost shortly after she began her employment at the establishment over eight years ago. She was putting fresh creamers on the tables at 6:00 AM when she looked to the front desk to see a soldier march through the restaurant carrying a gun as if he had business to attend to. Lillian said the transparent solider was about six feet tall, wore a soldier's hat and long trench coat as he quickly passed through. She later learned there were once US Army camps stationed nearby.

And as the owners of the establishment are proud to state, "The Gold Nugget Restaurant is so good, it's scary!"

Author's note: The Gold Nugget recently closed its kitchen in October 2016, but hopefully a new venue will reopen the doors and strike it rich in spirits soon!

Gold Nugget Restaurant & Lounge
222 East Wickenburg Way
Wickenburg, AZ 85390
928-684-0648

Navajo County

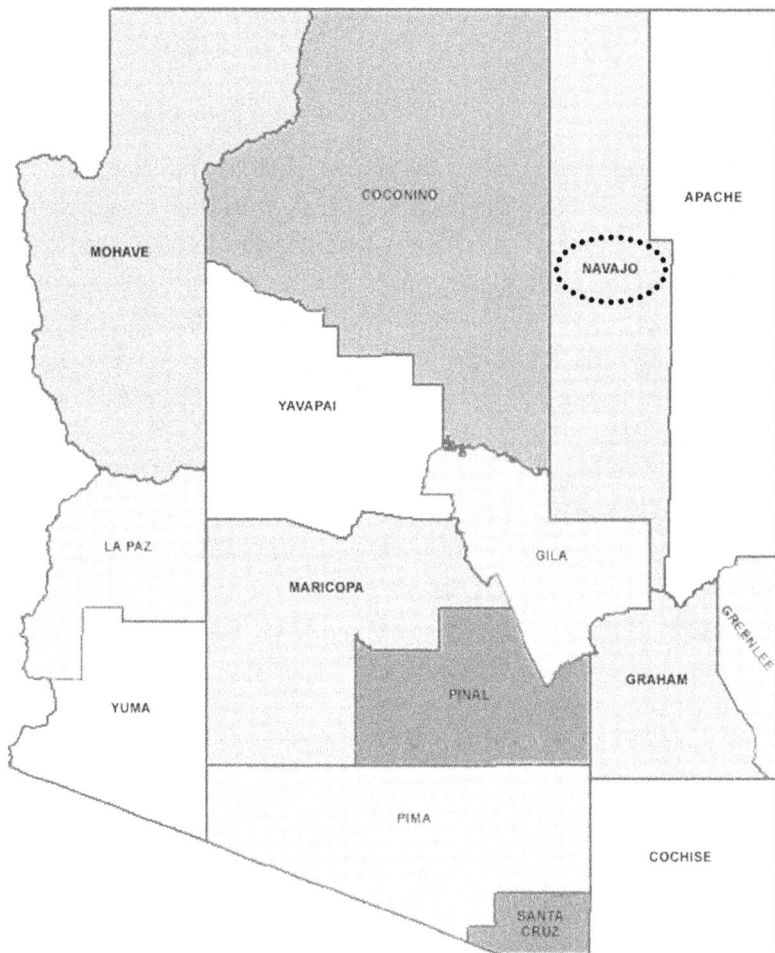

Bojo's Grill and Sports Club, Winslow

History

Bruchman's Trading Post opened in 1914 in Winslow, AZ. The trading post catered to the needs of members of the Navajo Nation who came to buy and to trade for merchandise to take back to the reservation. The trading post was run by an enterprising merchant named Robert M. Bruchman. His wife and family lived above the busy trading post. R. M. Bruchman loved the Navajo tribe, taking time to learn about their lives and traditions. He even wrote a booklet in 1923 called "Facts about the Navajos."

Everyone thought of Bruchman as a respected and trusted gentleman in the community. He often smoked fine cigars as he worked in his office doing inventory and the bookkeeping. Known for a witty sense of humor, he once had possession of a carcass of a supposed "Mermaid" at the trading post. He would tell customers the oddity was a member of a lost Navajo tribe and some traders actually believed him.

Bruchman's Trading Post was located on the popular Route 66 Highway and was always a stopping point for tourists who came to buy Navajo blankets and other Native American trinkets. As time marched on, the Navajos bought cars and trucks and started to go to supermarkets and department stores for their merchandise. The need for a trading post started to diminish. Bruchman's Trading Post continued as an outlet for Navajo crafts until 1995 when it closed its doors for good.

Today, the building houses Bojo's Grill & Sports Club. Bojo's provides delicious American cuisine for Winslow locals—as well for tourists who have come looking for a chance to stand on that famous "corner" from the Eagles' song "Take It Easy" just a block away.

Ghosts

The MVD Ghostchasers held their July 2006 Spirit Photography Workshop at the La Posada Hotel just a few blocks east of Bojo's Grill and Sports Club. They took the hungry crew of ghost hunters to Bojo's to grab a burger before their evening of paranormal investigations was about to begin. The group filled the dining area of the homestyle restaurant, and some of the group spilled over into the bar area and ordered their dinners from the bartender.

We asked the waitresses and bartenders to share some of the ghost stories experienced by the staff. They were happy to relate personal tales of encounters with Mr. Bruchman's ghost, who they feel still oversees the building.

"We call him Grandpa," they laughed. "He just gives you that warm feeling of a kind old man—like somebody's grandpa."

"And sometimes we smell the cigar smoke," the bartender added. "We can always tell when he is around because we smell the tobacco of a fine cigar."

They told us sometimes they hear noises as if someone is puttering around in the kitchen. Utensils and pans get moved from place to place. Sometimes they hear their names called out or whispers in their ears. They told us about a secret door in the kitchen that leads to underground tunnels. This was very exciting news. A small group of ghost hunters in the bar area listened intensely as the bartender explained that Chinese railroad workers had a network of tunnels running under the city of Winslow. As in many railroad towns, the Chinese dug the tunnels so they had a means of traveling about the neighborhoods without showing themselves on the street.

Workshop guest Sean volunteered to go into the tunnels, take a few pictures, and look for spirits or other paranormal activity lurking below. He was escorted to the kitchen area and descended down an old set of stairs that led him into total darkness. Armed with only a flashlight, he wandered through the catacombs snapping digital pictures as he fumbled through the pitch black pathway. He became a little unnerved and turned around—afraid he might make a wrong turn in the labyrinth and not find his way back to Bojo's kitchen. He was out of breath by the time he climbed back upstairs, and described the tunnels as something out of this world!

The next time you are dining at Bojo's and hear a whisper in your ear, remember it could be Mr. Bruchman doing his rounds at his former trading post. There might even be a hint of his cigar smoke lingering in the air—or better yet, the soothing aroma of a peace pipe from a Navajo trader of long ago.

Bojo's Grill and Sports Club
113 W. 2nd St.
Winslow, AZ 86047
928-289-0616
www.bojosgrill.com

Pima County

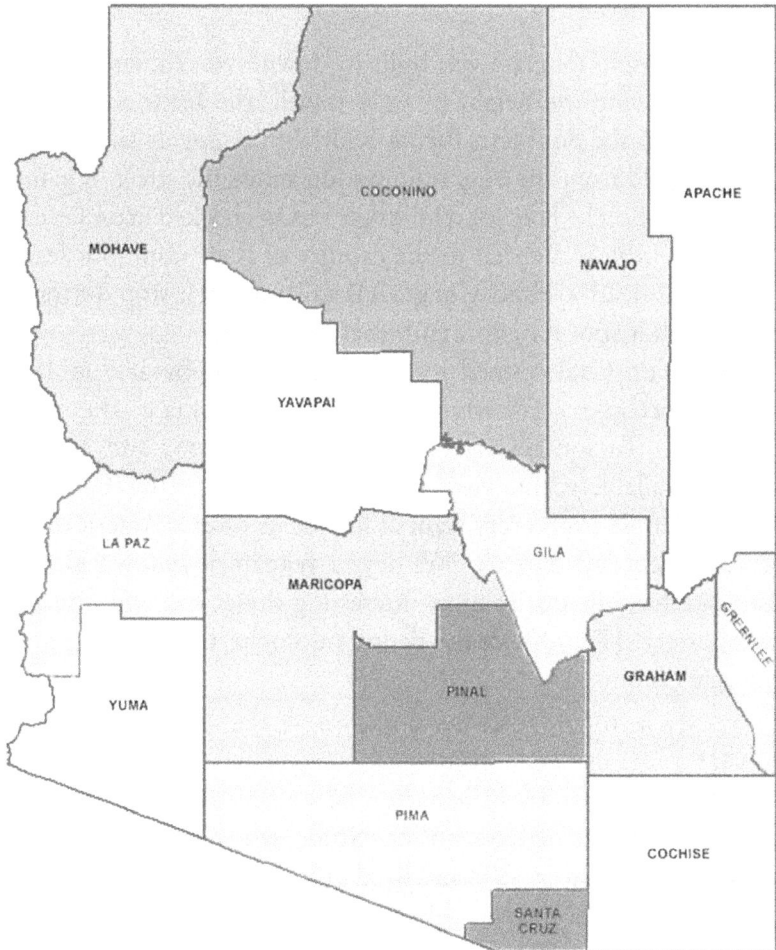

Cup Café, Tucson

History

The Hotel Congress was built in downtown Tucson, Arizona in 1919 during the height of train travel. The brick and marble hotel served the Southern Pacific Railroad passengers who arrived and departed from the busy train station across the street. It gained fame as the hotel where John Dillinger's gang checked in on January 21, 1934, which later led to the capture of their notorious leader hiding out nearby. Hotel Congress is still a popular stop for travelers and a hot spot for ghost enthusiasts.

The Cup Café opened just off the hotel lobby area in 1990 and has become a gathering spot for the residents of the swank downtown Tucson revival. There are both indoor and outdoor seating available with a very quaint Bristol-like setting. Cup Café attracts people from every walk of life for its diverse American fare served seven days a week, 365 days a year in downtown Tucson. The café has one of the most interesting floors you will find in a hotel eatery. 177,000 copper pennies decorate the floor in one of the café's rooms.

Ghosts

There is a friendly male entity the staff of the Hotel Congress and the Cup Café believes is Vince Szuda, who checked into Hotel Congress in the late 1950's and lived in Room 220 for a mere $7.00 a night. The hotel honored his bargain room rate until his passing on February 18, 2001. Vince was 84 years old when it is said he suffered a massive heart attack. Now his rent in the great beyond is free. His presence in the hotel is simply a friendly reminder of the man who once enjoyed residing there. While Vince doesn't bother the living, his apparition has been seen looking out the windows on the second floor, just enjoying the view of the city below.

When Vince was a resident of Hotel Congress, he used to constantly borrow the butter knives from the Cup Café. He would use them as makeshift screwdrivers in order to tinker around the hotel. He enjoyed tightening up the loose screws and bolts he found around the hallways in the historic hotel. When he was done with his impromptu maintenance work, he would simply place the butter knives in the hallway for the housekeeping staff to pick up later and return to the café. The hotel and restaurant staff believes Vince still keeps the hotel "ship shape" in the afterlife. They still find butter knives throughout the hotel hallways, lobby and café—just a friendly reminder that Vince Szuda is still among them taking pride in his former home.

Cup Café
311 E Congress St.
Tucson, AZ 85701
520-798-1618
www.hotelcongress.com/food

El Charro Café, Tucson

History

Tucson's El Charro Café was established in 1922 by Monica Flin. El Charro Café is the nation's oldest Mexican restaurant in continuous operation by the same family. Monica Flin came to Tucson via France in the 1800's when her father, a stone mason, was commissioned to build the city's pristine St. Augustine Cathedral.

He also built the family residence in 1896—now home to the original downtown El Charro Café on Court Avenue located in the heart of Tucson's historic El Presidio district. Designated on the National Register of Historic Places, the restaurant's high ceilings are made of black volcanic basalt rock which Jules Flin quarried from his claim at the foot of "A" Mountain.

Back in the old days, a female-owned business was rare indeed. El Charro was even more unique as it was truly a one-woman operation. Monica acted as hostess, waitress, and chef all at the same time. The restaurant moved around to a few locations and it finally landed in the old family home on Court Street in 1968. The décor's curios, tables, chairs, Mexican picture calendars, murals and saints' pictures are all from the original El Charro restaurant. Today Carlotta Dunn Flores, great grandniece of Monica, carries on the tradition of Tia Monica.

Tía Monica Flin is well known as "The Inventor of the Chimichanga." While frying some beef tacos, she accidently dropped a burro into the frying pan and when the oil splashed up, she was about to shout out a common Spanish cuss word starting with "Ch," but since she was in the same room with several nieces and nephews, she quickly changed it to "Chimichanga"—the equivalent of "thingamajig."

The word "Charro" is a name given to the peasants of the province Salamanca in Mexico. The word was adapted in 1857 and applied in Mexico to good, able horsemen. They are recognized by the costume or uniform they wear, especially the high-crowned, wide-brimmed hat.

Ghosts

The MVD Ghostchasers made their first visit to El Charro Café in 2000. The group had traveled to Tucson to visit a couple of local haunted hotels and began their evening with dinner at El Charro. They were seated in a private room that had a library setting. Throughout the dinner, they talked to staff members that had had ghostly encounters, and were left free to walk around the establishment and take photos.

The most common interaction the staff of the El Charro described with the spirits was a feeling of being watched or touched gently on the shoulder.

"It is as though someone is watching over the restaurant and guiding us to do the right thing for our customers," one of the waiters told the team.

Some of the staff say they have heard their names being called out, and others swear they have seen the image of an older woman appearing and disappearing right in front of them.

"Some believe Tía Monica is the one with the watchful eye over her restaurant," a longtime waiter told us.

Debe has dined at the café with other ghost hunter friends such as Karen Marchetti and Cindy Lee. Both times their waiters mentioned seeing unexplained things out of the corner of their eye, hearing their names called out, or having an odd feeling of being watched as they served the patrons.

Debe and Lisa Maureen Mustaca, one of the original MVD Ghostchasers, returned to El Charro Café to gather a few more stories for this chapter. It was a busy evening, so tracking down a staff member was a bit challenging.

A young waitress took a few minutes from her busy dinner guests to mention a story she had heard from the other staffers.

"We were having a meeting down in the basement where we always gather, and the subject of the ghosts had come up in the conversation," she said as she sat her tray down on a nearby table. "One of the staff said, 'I sometimes wonder if the original owners are here with us.' Another employee who was said to be intuitive smiled and said, 'Yes, they are! They are standing here laughing with us as we speak!' I know the ghosts are friendly, and we enjoy their presence."

El Charro Café is always in the center of action during Tucson's grand Día de los Muertos, or Day of the Dead, celebration and procession through the streets of the El Presidio. The area is decorated with sugar skulls, skeletons, and traditional Day of the Dead items. Dia de los Muertos is a day to celebrate, remember, and prepare special foods in honor of those who have departed. What better reason to dine with the dead at El Charro!

El Charro Café
311 N Court Avenue
Tucson, AZ 85701
520-622-1922
www.elcharrocafe.com

La Cocina Restaurant & Cantina, Tucson

History

La Cocina Restaurant is located in the heart of the historic El Presidio District of downtown Tucson and tucked inside the walls of the Old Town Artisans. Old Town Artisans is located on the site of El Presidio San Augustin del Tucson, the fort built by the Spanish in 1775 to stake claim to the northern frontier of New Spain. One block was the stables area, and the north wall is the location of the former fort's barrier from which Apache attacks were repelled. Construction of the adobe buildings began in the 1850's.

The 1882 Tucson Directory lists a variety of early residents, including assayers, clerks, a ladies' nurse and a grocery store. Many of the shops and businesses still have original ceilings made of saguaro cactus ribs, packing crates and whiskey barrel staves with remnants of imported wallpaper and gold-leaf moldings.

The beautiful lighted courtyard restaurant of La Cocina boasts al fresco dining, a rustic cantina, and live music under the stars.

Ghosts

Jo Schneider is the current owner of the La Cocina Restaurant and Cantina, and spends the evening mingling with her guests making sure their dining experience is memorable.

Jo reported that many employees and patrons of the restaurant have seen an apparition of a cowboy dressed in chaps and a duster standing on the stairs that descend into the courtyard dining area. Sometimes his silhouette is seen standing along the outside walls of the nearby shops and his noisy boot steps are heard pacing about the courtyard.

Some members of the restaurant staff refuse to be left alone in the facility after dark.

"The staff was closing out the cash drawers one evening when the calculators all started to run on their own," Jo told us. "This area was once the land of an early Hohokam village. Later it became the site of the busy El Presidio settlement of old Tucson with brothels, stables, and merchants. The energy is very rich throughout this entire plaza." Guests that visit the plaza have reported being touched, seeing the apparition of the cowboy, and even one of a little girl. Some have experienced setting an item down somewhere only to find it in an entirely different location. The ghosts like to play!

The website "Tucson Museum" tells the story of Craig Chester, a gentleman who worked at the La Cocina Restaurant. He claims he has seen a ghost not once, but twice. "I was kind of standing there and saw something out of the corner of my eye and I looked over there to the corner of the room and there's an old man standing there. I've never seen a ghost before in my life. It was my first time. To see a ghost twice kind of verifies that these spirits do hang around," stated Chester.

Ghost tour guide Becky Gydesen says of La Cocina, "It's very active…very active." Gydesen invites her tour to sit down in the gallery inside La Cocina where they use various pieces of paranormal equipment to try to communicate with the spirits.

The Tucson Ghost Experience Tour is a great way to experience the ghosts at La Cocina. One tour guest said, "My friends and I are very much into the paranormal and decided to do a ghost hunt with the Tucson Ghost Experience Tour. It took place at La Cocina Restaurant, where our group had the place to ourselves after hours. Some equipment was provided for us to use around the place, which was an added bonus. While we didn't see anything visually, we did catch some strange and unexplained sounds during our EVP session. Some of our equipment went off at certain times and we couldn't figure out why. I, personally, plan on going back a few times to see if we might catch something on camera."

Gydesen added, "We heard some dragging sounds at the La Cocina when we held our recent 'locked down' ghost investigation. We also heard a bell ringing as though someone was entering the building. The calculator in the restaurant office goes off like crazy with the paper spitting out random numbers. I was also touched on the shoulder while doing a tour in the gallery area."

Interested in a ghost tour that includes the La Cacina? They meet at the La Cocina Restaurant at the corner of Court and Washington. Have a bite to eat and be sure to reserve your spot on the ghost tour. Contact www.tucsonghosttour.com for more information.

La Cocina Restaurant & Cantina
201 N Court Avenue
Tucson, AZ 85701
520-622-0351
www.lacocinatucson.com

Li'l Abner's Steakhouse, Tucson

History

Li'l Abner's was first established as a Butterfield Overland Express stage stop in the early 1800's. The building was also used as a ranch style residence and an eyeglass factory for short periods of time. But for the majority of years since 1947, the rustic building has continuously operated as a restaurant and bar. It is located in a scenic rural setting on old Silverbell Road, an approximately 15-minute drive from downtown Tucson.

Li'l Abner's is an authentic old-time western bar and restaurant filled with memorabilia of southwestern history. It features an expansive patio with wood picnic tables and benches. Indoors, the décor is Western and to the point!

It has long been a hot spot for cowboys in the rural setting between Marana and Tucson. The clientele also included tourists from the neighboring guest ranches and Tucson's Gem and Mineral Show. It was not uncommon for music stars like Kris Kristofferson and Treat Williams to pop into the bar and play with the house bands.

Ghosts

The most prominent ghost of Li'l Abner's Steakhouse is not from the Old West history of the restaurant, but is said to be from the 1990's and was a former employee of the establishment. They call the ghost "George." George was an elderly black gentleman who was once the maintenance man at the restaurant. He lived in a small house in the rear of the restaurant, which still stands today. A small wooden sign hangs over the doorway that reads "George's." George, keeping up with his good work ethic, does not bother the diners, and is considered a terribly shy ghost.

Employees at Li'l Abner's have seen the ghost of George and have heard what they believe is his voice, too. George was known to take frequent jaunts down to old Mexico, but before he would set out on his journey, he would always stop and drink a large Coke at the bar. Some employees have seen George dressed in white, standing at the bar and sipping away at his large glass of Coke, only to witness him disappearing a few moments later. Some of the staff has heard items falling behind the bar or their names being called out only to turn around and find themselves all alone near the barstools.

Another known habit of George's was his love of Cap'n Crunch Cereal. People have heard a "crunching" sound inside the restaurant kitchen or from within the walls of his old maintenance room as though he was still enjoying a bowl of his favorite breakfast cereal.

There are stories of other ghosts that haunt this building. Muffled conversations or whispered voices are heard. There has been knocking on doors only to find nobody standing on the other side of the door.

Ghost hunters Lisa Mustaca and Debe Branning stopped in at Li'l Abner's to gather a few new ghost stories. Walking onto the roomy patio area, they stopped to talk to one of the cooks as he placed several steaks onto the large grill.

"There is a little girl ghost here, too," he told us. "I don't know if she was from the stagecoach days, or lived here when it was the ranch. But she seems to be around early in the morning when it is quiet and only a few of us are here. We hear her singing or giggling at us."

Another employee came outside and he added, "It's true. One day I was here early cleaning up and thought I heard a girl singing on the radio…only the radio was not even turned on. It was a little girl's voice!"

We went inside to talk to Connie, the longtime owner and manager of Li'l Abner's. Connie was excited to talk about the ghosts of her establishment, including George.

"He was quite the character!" she said with a giggle.

Connie pointed to a table located close to a wall adorned with photos of Wyatt Earp and other Old West icons. The table, covered with a red and white checkered tablecloth, seats six guests.

"One evening we had three couples that had just spent the day at the Gem and Mineral Show and came to our restaurant for a steak dinner," Connie recalled. "They had ordered their meals and were enjoying appetizers when one of the ladies let out a little shriek and jumped up from her chair. She swore that someone grabbed her around the waist from behind, but nobody in her group witnessed anyone in the restaurant standing behind her."

Both Connie and the bartender have seen the chairs pulled out away from this same table late at night after everything had been put in its place after closing.

"Someone must really like this spot," Connie shook her head.

Connie mentioned that she was there late one night when a different maintenance employee passed away. "We were standing in the room where the band plays when we suddenly heard a loud, painful moan. The next morning we learned our employee had died at that exact same time."

Connie believes all of her ghosts at Li'l Abner's are the friendly sort. "I was sitting here at the end of the bar (close to the haunted table of six) late one night thinking about the history of the building and our ghostly friends. All of a sudden the neon Dr. Pepper sign blinked on and off by itself. It was almost like they were acknowledging the fact that they were still here.

Another ghost dates from when the building was used as an eyeglass factory. They say this spirit is an ex-factory worker who is still looking for his lost eyeglasses, so be careful where you place your eyewear during dinner.

Step back into early Arizona history and enjoy a delicious meal at one of Tucson's landmarks. Stop in for a spell, and be sure to order a large Coke and make a toast to George!

Li'l Abner's Steakhouse
8501 North Silverbell Rd.
Tucson, AZ 85743
520-744-2800

Maynards Market and Kitchen/ Tucson Historic Train Depot, Tucson

History

The sleepy railroad depot in Tucson, Arizona became the scene of a western shootout back on March 22, 1882 when Wyatt Earp shot outlaw Frank Stilwell dead near the platform. The mourning Earp clan was taking the body of Morgan Earp on the train back to California for burial. Ike Clanton and Frank Stilwell hid at the depot waiting to ambush and overtake the grieving brothers. Instead, Stilwell became the one destined for death. Wyatt Earp fired a shot point blank under Stilwell's ribs. Witnesses said several shots were heard in the train yard, and they found Stilwell's body riddled with bullets several hours later.

The current railroad station was built in 1941 and was in use during the heyday of rail travel in the 1940's and 1950's. The building was boarded up and forgotten during the 1970's. In 1998, the City of Tucson purchased the Southern Pacific Depot from the Union Pacific Railroad, and the depot was placed on the National Register of Historic Places. The building now houses an Amtrak station with some of the beautiful original 1942 wood furniture pieces in use. There is also a market, a train museum, and a romantic restaurant on the premises called Maynards.

Ghosts

Wyatt Earp has said Stilwell's last words were *"Morg? Morg?"* perhaps mistaken that he had encountered the ghost of Morgan Earp. Morgan and Wyatt Earp looked somewhat alike. Stilwell's ghost has been reportedly seen wandering in the area of the old platform and railroad station that stood near the Southern Pacific tracks of days gone by. Some ghost hunters have even recorded EVP's of mysterious gunfire while investigating the area.

I stopped and talked to one of the Amtrak security guards to learn if he had witnessed any ghostly activity, since he is alone in the Amtrak station on many occasions. He admitted that several of the security personnel had witnessed a man in a territorial military uniform who vanished as they approached him. They have also heard a woman scream from the restroom. Thinking there might be a lady in distress; they checked the room and found nobody there. They believe it could be the rumored ghost of a runaway who was found raped, murdered, and left along the tracks in the 1970's. An apparition of a tattered bloody man has been seen near the stairway, as well as a grieving woman in black wandering in the area of the train station.

The old Number 1673 locomotive is housed in a fenced area near the train museum. It seems to carry a little energy from its past as well. Once used in the 1954 movie *Oklahoma*, the engine seems to attract a misty green haze in photos. Ghost hunters have seen a middle-aged conductor standing nearby just gazing at the old iron horse.

Nancy Marine and I explored both the downstairs and upstairs dining areas of the restaurant, Maynards. Our waiter informed us that workers in the market have reported seeing wine bottles rise up in the air and crash to the tile floor. Strange odors from the basement have been known to filter up to the main floor. There was once a jail cell in the basement for holding prisoners being transported by train to other facilities.

Railroad travel and the depots were once as busy and hectic as the city airports are now. Men road trains off to war. Their loved ones rode the rails to the coasts to greet the soldiers when they returned on the ships. Many diseased travelers rode the trains to Arizona with hopes of recovering from illnesses and never returned to their former homes. No wonder there are so many emotions, energies and apparitions left behind in the station and the area now used as the restaurant.

Maynards Market and Kitchen
400 N Toole Avenue
Tucson, AZ 85701
520-545-0577
www.maynardstucson.com

Pinal County

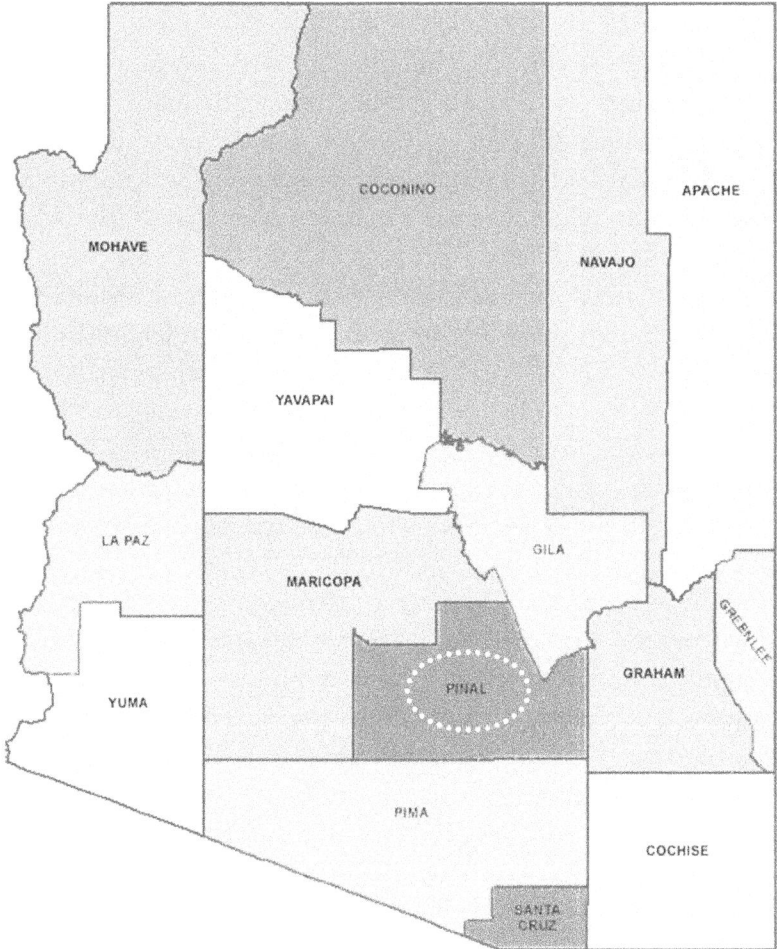

Dirtwater Springs, Apache Junction

History

Take a drive to the East Valley's Apache Junction area and enjoy lunch or dinner at a rustic looking restaurant called Dirtwater Springs. It should fill your appetite just as it served weary travelers and their vehicles back in the early days when it was known as a gasoline filling station—the Superstition Mountain Shell Station along the Apache Trail.

What some people don't know is that the former Shell station was the scene of a grisly robbery which led to a murder nearby back on December 29, 1947. Julian and Lucy King had begun construction on King's Guest Ranch near the area of Gold Canyon. During the summer of 1947, they gave Angel "Rocky" Serna a job. The couple knew Serna was an ex-convict, but his probation officer, a friend of the Kings, assured them Serna was ready to go straight and hold down a job.

Rocky helped the Kings put in the water system at the guest ranch and was a valuable employee throughout the entire summer. Sometimes Rocky would go into town on the weekends, and got to know several of the owners of the local businesses. It was during this time that Rocky became interested in horses and wanted to own his own racehorse.

In September of 1947, Rocky found a racehorse he was interested in buying, but the horse was priced at $400—more money than Rocky had on hand. He didn't know how he was going to raise that amount of money in such a short time. The Kings tried to explain to Rocky that $400 was too much money to spend on a horse. Rocky insisted he could raise the money for the horse and quit his job at King's Ranch. He took on employment in Apache Junction at the end of October 1947.

He spent a good deal of the morning of December 29, 1947 at the Apache Junction Inn. Later he took a trip down to the Superstition Mountain Shell Station, where he was going to try to borrow the $400 for the horse from the owner—Katherine M. Gohn. To his dismay, Mrs. Gohn was not at the station.

Rocky left but returned a short time later. With the owner still away from the business, he wandered in and out of the station and finally came up with a wild plan to rob the place. Rocky went to steal a pistol, then headed back to the Superstition Mountain Shell Station and demanded money at gunpoint.

Fairy Thompson, daughter of Katherine Gohn, knew Rocky and thought he was just joking around—that is, until he shot her in the chest. Thompson's two young daughters ran out a back door to get help for their mother.

After shooting Fairy Thompson, Rocky stomped over to the nearby home of Katherine Gohn. He shot Mrs. Gohn in the hand, and then dragged her into a bedroom where he raped and shot her in the head. He stole her car and headed east on Highway 60. For some reason he turned up King's Ranch Road and got stuck in a wash.

Serna walked to King's Guest Ranch and approached a man, asking him for a ride to Safford. Rocky told the man he had just killed two women. The frightened man refused to help, and Serna wandered down the road on foot.

The incident was immediately reported to the Pinal County Sheriff's Office. Serna was quickly apprehended by a Chandler constable and a Highway Patrolman and booked into Pinal County Jail in Florence. Gohn was found dead—but her daughter survived her injuries. Serna was convicted of murder in the first degree and executed in Arizona's new gas chamber on July 29, 1950.

Ghosts

Now guests and employees of Dirtwater Springs are visited by ghosts—particularly the spirit of Katherine Gohn. One of the young waitresses reported that she was doing some prep work in the kitchen before her shift began. She heard what sounded like the muffled voice of a woman speaking. Then she felt someone swoosh past behind her, bumping into her long ponytail, and a chilling breeze rushed by. Other waitresses have seen shadows in the kitchen and have felt the temperature drop, too.

The bar in the front dining area has had its share of ghostly action as well. Glasses have been seen flying off the shelves, and other items have moved about the bar front. This was most likely the area of the front counter of the old gas station. There have been times when employees have heard a ghostly echo of the old familiar dinging sound of the bell that alerted the gas attendant when a customer pulled up to the gas pumps.

Another active spot in the restaurant is the ladies' restroom. Years ago, one of the waitresses saw a woman with a blank expression on her face as she entered the unlocked door to the restroom. She asked the woman if she need some assistance and was baffled as the woman suddenly faded away.

Another one of the young waitresses reported hearing the sliding lock of the bathroom door clicking into place as she stood at the mirror brushing her hair before her shift began. She also felt the cool breeze of an unseen presence. She glanced down at the latch, noticed it was still unlocked, and immediately left the bathroom.

Paranormal teams such as the Crossing Over Paranormal Society and the MVD Ghostchasers have visited Dirtwater Springs with the intent to prove or disprove tales of the hauntings. A medium with Crossing Over Paranormal Society noted a lady dressed in white in the supposedly haunted restroom.

Employees say they have also seen the ghost they believe is Katherine Gohn wandering about the restaurant after closing time. With all of these reported sightings of a ghostly lady—one can only wonder if Katherine is still attending to her bustling Superstition Mountain Shell Station, wanting to give the best service possible.

Dirtwater Springs
586 W Apache Trail
Apache Junction, AZ 85120
480-983-3478
www.dirtwatersprings.com

Café de Manuel, Casa Grande

History

Café de Manuel opened its doors in 1995 and is located in Casa Grande, Arizona. It has been reported that the restaurant was built on a location that was once a residential home built about 1965, and later became a 7-11 or Circle K convenience market store. It is now a popular Mexican food restaurant that offers live music on weekends.

The current owners, Torres & Cortes LLC, purchased the property from Christine, the wife of the original owner of Café de Manuel, Phillip W Glenn, six years after his death in 2002. They strive to carry on the same fine quality of food and service as their predecessor, making Café de Manuel a must for local Arizonans craving that South of the Border experience.

Ghosts

There have been many reports of Café de Manuel employees seeing the original owners of the former residence in the building. An elderly woman (perhaps a former home owner) has been seen in different areas of the restaurant. There is also the ghost of a male, perhaps the convenience store employee that is said to have been shot and murdered during a botched robbery attempt.

One of the managers noted that several patrons of the restaurant sitting on the outdoor patio have described seeing a phantom dog walking through the enclosed area. Other diners have seen what they believe are apparitions of the previous cafe owners. It is said that Mr. Glenn had a great love for his restaurant.

The kitchen staff does not like being alone in the restaurant late at night. They have reported hearing the clanging of pots and pans in the kitchen, as well as other strange or unexplainable sounds.

They have witnessed some of the hanging cooking utensils fall off the wall for no explainable reason.

In November 2007, a couple of Arizona paranormal teams decided to investigate Café de Manuel to see if they could prove or disprove the hauntings reported over the years. Southern Arizona Scientific Paranormal Investigators (SASPI) arrived on the scene looking for answers. It was their first investigation and the team was anxious to interview the employees who were working at the time. Some of the employees told them they often felt cold spots and saw things out of the corners of their eyes. They also believed that the spirit of the woman who used to live there still roamed the property.

David E. Chavez, a member of SASPI, described his experience at the Mexican venue.

"When we did the investigation, I had felt a cold spot about where the store clerk had been reportedly shot. I was sitting at a table with my back against the wall when I suddenly saw what looked like a bright orange ball of light floating and suddenly disappear. The best I can describe it is that it looked like a Jawa's (Star Wars) eye. Whenever we would go to the restaurant, I sat at the same table where I saw the orb. I would feel a little uneasy, a little dizzy, or sick to my stomach. I also felt a dog running through the dining area—but I don't recall feeling or seeing the female spirit. I have also sat at the table between the fountain and the patio and felt a presence."

Another paranormal team, West Coast GAPS, also paid a visit to the Café De Manuel in November 2007. The manager and staff told the team they had seen knives fall from a magnetic board and objects fall from a top shelf in a utility room. The manager also mentioned that several patrons sitting in the patio area have seen what they describe as a phantom dog walking through the enclosed area. These same witnesses also believe that some apparitions from the property's past have also been sighted from time to time.

West Coast GAPS conducted their investigation from 9:30pm until 1:00am on November 10, 2007. The team located high EMF readings in the kitchen, which could account for the employees' uneasy feelings of being watched. The utensils could have easily fallen off the magnetic board if someone mortal bumped up against the adjoining wall.

They believe the "ghost dog" could be owed to window placements that allowed for unique shadows and reflections from passing cars. West Coast GAPS stated "They had no personal experiences or evidence upon reviewing audio, video or photos."

Despite the skepticism of GAPS, no one can say for sure just who is behind the ghostly activity and if the spirit is still around—or perhaps in hiding. Some of the employees still won't work in the kitchen alone at night. Even though it's scary, they sometimes chat about the tragic tale of the dearly departed convenience store clerk and wonder if someday he will return.

Café De Manuel Mexican Food
1300 North Pinal Avenue
Casa Grande, AZ 85122
520-421-3199

Lupita's Mexican Food, Casa Grande

History

Constructed in 1907, this small adobe building has been the home to many businesses and restaurants through the years. The energies left behind by some proprietors and customers could be the reason for the activity reported by paranormal investigators.

The original purpose of the building was that of a general store known as Johnston's Grocery Store, and later it became the Casa Grande Market. The small market served the Casa Grande area for many years. George Washington Johnston purchased the store and added clothing and dry goods along with the groceries.

On July 9, 1935, the storekeeper was working in the rear room of the store when two men entered the establishment. What was supposed to be a simple robbery turned into vicious homicide. They brutally beat Mr. Johnston with a pipe and robbed the store register of $13.00. A customer, who had come in the store to make a purchase, found Mr. Johnston barely conscious and lying in the back room. He summoned help and Johnston was taken to the local hospital. He was too critically injured, and he died the next morning.

Eventually, the two assailants were captured and one of the men confessed. They were both tried and convicted. The one who struck the fatal blow received the gas chamber, and the other received life in prison.

Many say the spirit of G. W. Johnston lingers in the old adobe.

From 1940 through 1955, the building was utilized as one of the first self-service laundromats of Casa Grande and the area. In the 1960's the laundry service was replaced with a restaurant called Sophia's. It has changed owner's hands several times in recent years; it became the Casa Grande Café, and most recently it operated as Lupita's Mexican Food.

Ghosts

Most of the former restaurant owners and their wait staff will agree that there are ghostly phenomena associated with the building. The workers said when they walked through certain areas of the kitchen, it was hard to concentrate. On several occasions they had to stop and rethink on what they had come to do or look for in the kitchen. They witnessed pots and pans flying off the shelves and landing with a crash in a completely different area of the kitchen.

Most of them agreed there was a spirit in the back room. No one had actually seen the ghost, but its presence was felt and many employees said there was uneasiness—as though they were being watched. One server stated he felt cold and often had goose bumps any time he went to the back room to grab napkins or other supplies.

The dining area has had its encounters with the spirits as well. An old man has been seen sitting in one of the red booths. Many think it is the former store proprietor, Mr. G. W. Johnston. The spirit is dressed in outdated clothing and sports long sideburns on his face.

Past employees told stories of seeing the man sitting in the booth observing the other patrons in the building. Mr. Johnston could still be checking on the store he loved so dearly and managed for nearly thirty years. The wait staff carefully approached the booth before reaching for their tips, because the gentleman ghost has appeared at the table, frightening them on many occasions.

Past servers say they have seen filled water glasses glide across tables and crash to the floor as if someone had given the vessels a gentle push. They claim other objects have fallen off the walls and tables, or are playfully moved about the restaurant.

MVD Ghostchasers Debe, Lisa McDaniel and Megan Taylor dined in "Mr. Johnson's booth" the evening of their mini-investigation of the restaurant. They set out an extra place setting and menu in Johnston's spot, hoping he would join them for dinner. The investigators continued to converse with the spot in the booth where we hoped our special ghostly guest was seated. At one point, the hair raised on Lisa's right arm and she glanced quickly at the empty seating beside her.

"I felt a cold spot for just a minute," she said as she rubbed her arm.

We snapped a few pictures with the digital cameras, hoping for a glimpse of the ghostly patron. Then we saw a napkin fall to the floor. One of us might have bumped the cotton cloth napkin, but on the other hand, maybe the ghost was enjoying the company of the three female ghost hunters. Either way, we recommend you request the quiet booth in the dining room and asked to be seated next to the elderly gentleman with the friendly smile.

Author's note: At this time, Lupita's Mexican Food is closed but the historic building still stands, holding its spirits.

Lupita's Mexican Food
301 N Picacho St.
Casa Grande, AZ 85122
520-836-1244

Gallopin' Goose Saloon & Grill, Coolidge

History

The "Goose" has been a Coolidge, Arizona icon since 1935. Its neon sign still draws guests in nightly to the country music honky-tonk. Regulars can only imagine how many beers have gone down there—along with new romances, broken hearts, and weekend brawls. The Gallopin' Goose bar was once the hangout for country music star Waylon Jennings in the 1960's.

Jennings' career started in 1958 when he became a member of Buddy Holly's group The Crickets. On February 3, 1959, while touring with Holly, the Big Bopper and Ritchie Valens, Jennings gave up his seat on the ill-fated plane to the Big Bopper. After Holly's untimely death, Jennings moved to Coolidge. The local watering hole claim to fame is that Waylon sat in with a local band and joined them on tour. He later took off on his own and made a name for himself at clubs in the Phoenix area. Jennings also worked as a radio DJ in Coolidge around 1959 at KCKY on Main Street. He was known as "Sky High Jennings" on the air, but it was his talent as a performer that later took him to the top of the country music industry. The Gallopin' Goose has a small wall of Waylon Jennings photos and memorabilia–the Waylon Wall as they call it. Waylon Jennings is buried in the City of Mesa Cemetery.

Ghosts

Does the ghost of Waylon Jennings haunt the Gallopin' Goose? Paranormal investigator Dianne Golding and her paranormal group, Arizona Phantom Paranormal Society, were determined to find out. Along with team members Dianne Loughin and Jeff Nichols, they made arrangements to do an investigation of the Gallopin' Goose on a Sunday night after the bar closed.

The owners and staff were quick to point out some of the unusual happenings that had occurred through the years, including the mop bucket that moved across the floor under its own power.

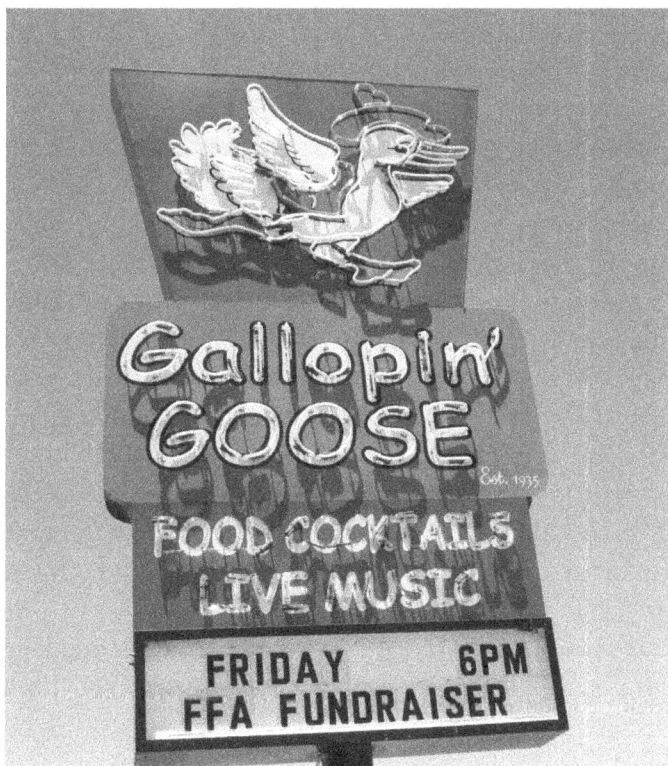

During their investigation, nothing out of the ordinary seemed to occur. However, upon reviewing their video tape evidence, they discovered there was more than met the eye! Their first piece of evidence occurred when Dianne walked past the video camera that was busy recording inside the bar near the stage area. You can hear someone whispering, "Don't worry; I'm not going to touch you."

Dianne walked over and sat down at a booth a little later and had to sneeze. You can clearly hear someone say, "Bless you." She walked around the area a little more and chose to sit down at yet another booth. Dianne pulled out a small silver flashlight, and later, she was surprised she could hear a voice on her audio recorder say, "It's a lollipop," which could easily refer to the style of microphone that Waylon Jennings would have used during the early years of his performances at the Gallopin' Goose.

Finally, during a review of the video tape, the team noted a strange light flash across the leg of one of the pool tables. There were no lights flashing in the bar that night, and it only did it once during the entire 2 1/2 hours the team performed their paranormal investigation.

The wait staff at the Gallopin' Goose reported seeing the dark shadowy image of a cowboy standing at the doorway that opens up to the kitchen. The phantom cowboy is usually seen leaning on the door frame with one leg propped on the woodwork.

One of the waitresses stated she heard a stack of dishes fall onto the kitchen floor while she was in the dining area cleaning up after the bar had closed. When she dashed back to the kitchen to investigate, she found the dishes stacked neatly in a pile in another area of the room.

Almost all of the wait staff agreed that the dance floor is the eeriest spot in the old honkytonk. "A lot has gone on in that room throughout the years and I guess some of the energies have chosen to linger on."

And who knows, maybe Waylon Jennings pops onto the stage from time to time still looking for that "Good Hearted Woman."

Gallopin' Goose Saloon & Grill
1980 S Arizona Blvd.
Coolidge, AZ 85128
520-723-0300
www.gallopingoosesaloon.com

Yavapai County

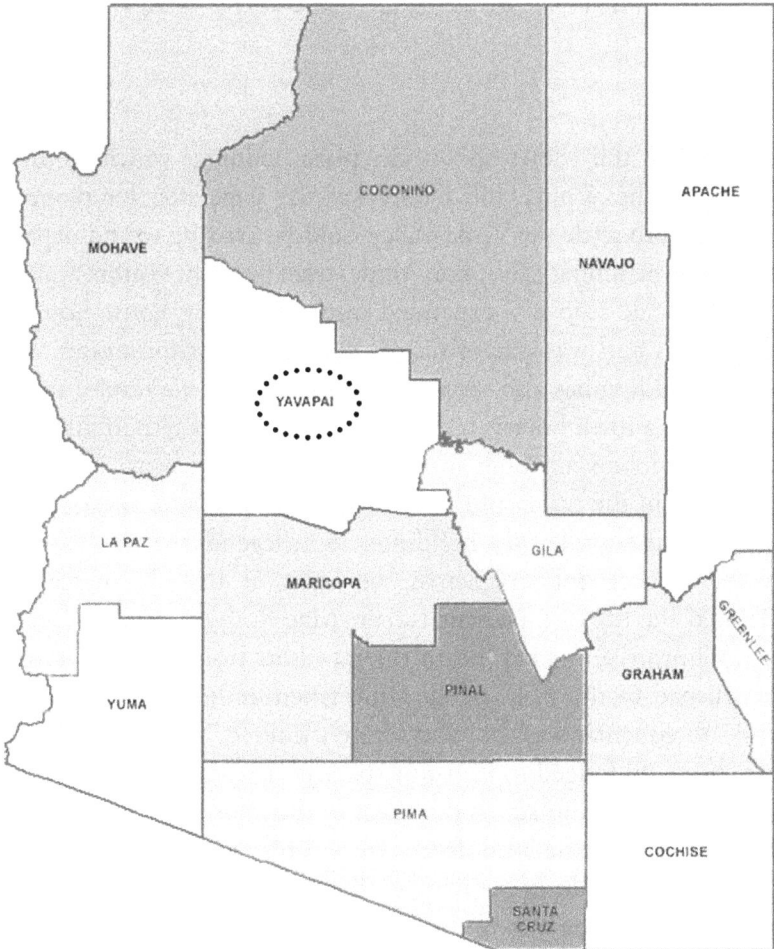

Adobe Cafe aka Cowboy Cuisine BBQ, Camp Verde

History

Built in the 1860's-1870's, the plaza buildings which are now known as the White Hills Court was the stage stop for pioneers coming in to settle the Verde Valley. Soldiers arriving to and departing from the military fort, Fort Verde, were frequent visitors as well.

The stage stop was expanded into a boarding house/hotel in the 1870's and was one of Camp Verde's earliest businesses. The adobe building has also served as a business office, a home, a dentist office, a town library, retail stores, and various restaurants. The original adobe walls built in the 1800's still hold firm. There is a huge tree in the center of the adobe plaza that shades and protects the patrons as well as the building and its legends.

A botched robbery across the street at the old mercantile claimed the life of merchant Robert Mac Rodgers. Rodgers' partner, Clinton Wingfield, heard the gunshots from the back room. He rushed to the front of the store when he heard all the noise, and subsequently was shot and severely injured. The bullet entered his chest and lodged in his spine, paralyzing him almost instantly. Friends carried him across the street to the main room of the stage stop depot, and the local doctor treated his wounds. He died two hours later in front of the fireplace in the building that later would serve as the dining area of the Cowboy Cuisine/Adobe Cafe.

Ghosts

My ghost hunting friends, The Verde Valley Spirit Seekers, up in Camp Verde, AZ contacted me with news that activity was at a new high at the White Hills Court plaza. We had previously done an investigation at the site when the Adobe Cafe was in business and owned by Barbie Bridge. Now White Hills Court was undergoing a major transformation. Ginger Mason, a longtime merchant in the plaza (and a member of Verde Valley Spirit Seekers) was closing out her trading post/jewelry business. At the same time, a new restaurant called the Cowboy Cuisine BBQ, owned by Lori Webster, was having its grand opening.

Were the ghosts simply confused? Or were they simply having a difficult time adjusting to changes like many of us do in our daily lives? Deb Wilber sent me an invitation to grab a couple of investigators and make the trip up north to work with their four-member team. Cindy Lee also took the bait, and we headed to Camp Verde on a late Saturday afternoon.

Previously, The MVD Ghostchasers had held an April 2007 workshop in Camp Verde. At the time, Barbie Bridge was the owner of the former Adobe Café and agreed to speak to the group about the ghosts she had witnessed while operating the café. Barbie reported seeing a tall elderly cowboy standing by the large tree in the courtyard patio. His appearance was brief, fading away almost as quickly as he had appeared.

"I have seen the image of a round-toed Calvary boot entering the kitchen and disappearing when I went in to take a better look," Barbie added, pointing to the kitchen area of the cafe.

More recently, we met Deb, Ginger, Devon Artrip, and the late Judy Valencia at the restaurant and enjoyed a delicious BBQ dinner provided by Cowboy Cuisine. Current owner Lori sat down with us in the courtyard patio and described some of the events that had been happening since she took proprietorship of the building.

Lori added a few new ghost stories to the growing list. She had no idea there were spirits lurking in her cafe when purchasing the building in March 2009. But unexplained things began to happen just three days after opening up for business.

Doors began to open and close, open and close, over and over again. One morning Lori was alone in the cafe. She was reaching for cooking utensils on a high shelf. Standing on tippy toes, she stretched to grab the items on the top ledge. She suddenly felt a hand touch her shoulder as if to hold her body steady so she would not fall. She turned around to find a shadowlike figure standing between her and an exit door. Sometimes items fell off shelves in the kitchen that were tucked away near the back wall. Once, her mini food processor flew across the room.

Lori had one experience similar to what former Adobe Cafe owner Barbie witnessed. She heard the back door open, and moments later she heard boot steps entering the room. She did not see the boots, but she could hear the heavy footsteps walking towards her. Lori said she was a little apprehensive another day when she was in the hallway and a shadowy figure passed her. All she remembered seeing was a man's backside and back of his legs… and then he was gone.

For the most part Lori believed the ghosts were very comforting. She felt the spirit of a woman standing near the stove watching her. The Cowboy Cuisine was pretty active during the daytime and the night.

The Verde Valley Spirit Seekers have filmed shadows and unexplained phenomena in the courtyard patio outside the various shops on several occasions. They have also felt the presence of a ghost in the eerie courtyard. Barbie and ghost hunter Ginger, have both seen an apparition of a woman sitting in a chair along the wall of the adobe courtyard. Team member, Judy, witnessed the shadow of a man walking in a fast pace along side of the adobe building and disappeared into the walls.

On the evening of the ghost hunt, we had every camera angle covered. Cameras pointed in all directions out on the patio. As Cindy was setting up her camera on the fireplace mantel, she saw a shadow move behind her as she was looking into the digital camera screen.

The group also spotted other curious shadows lurking in the hallway and the back storage rooms. We aimed the cameras in that direction and took turns doing EVP sessions. About 3:00 AM we crawled into sleeping bags sprawled across the floor in Ginger's old shop.

When in Camp Verde be sure to stop at this historic plaza. It was once buzzing with early settlers and some of their spirits are still visiting the stage stop to fulfill their transcendent travels. You just might find that great photo opportunity to capture a true apparition on video or with your digital camera.

At this time there is no business occupying this location. You can still visit the patio area. Bring your own lunch and perhaps you will experience spirits passing through as they wait for the next stagecoach.

Contact Deb Wilbur at "Verde Valley Spirit Seekers" for the latest stories about the Adobe Café.

Adobe Cafe aka Cowboy Cuisine BBQ
567 S. Main St.
Camp Verde, AZ 86322

Wild Rose of Historic Old Town Tea House, Cottonwood

History

This quaint Wild Rose of Historic Old Town Tea House was once the notorious Cottonwood Jail. The building was largely constructed of river cobbles in 1929 and first occupied by a local judge in 1930. The cells were originally part of a Navy brig, and lifted by crane into the jail. Over the years it grew in size, adding on cells, then rooms, and soon the number of prisoners it could hold began to increase. The jail held only two cells made of steel, which would bake a man alive during the hot, sunny Arizona days of summer.

During prohibition, Cottonwood was the perfect setting for the overflow of bootleggers and criminal acts associated with trafficking illegal booze. The jail would house up to twenty people, ten on each side, during the Prohibition era.

The Cottonwood police department used it as their town jail for several years. Joe Hall was named "Arizona's King Bootlegger" and was the first to be jailed in the new facility. He was known to have spent a good deal of time incarcerated in the jail. Many locals claim there was some sort of a Joe Hall/Al Capone bootlegging trade connection. Some say Al Capone stopped at the jail to take care of some business with Joe Hall and carved his name on the side wall of one of the jail cells during the visit.

During Prohibition, many local Native Americans were arrested for public intoxication and housed in the tiny jail, sometimes up to twelve in a cell. Occasionally the guards would find that one of the inmates had hanged himself in the overcrowded cells with a piece of clothing during the night

Even as recent as sometime between 1960 and 1970, a young man is said to have committed suicide in the jail by hanging himself. His distraught girlfriend later walked down to the nearby Verde River and hanged herself as well.

Visitors are invited to enjoy a late continental breakfast or specialty teas, and then take a stroll through the old jail cells to photograph Capone's name carved upon the wall.

Ghosts

Due to the large quantities of prisoners often packed within the confined jail space on busy Cottonwood nights, it is presumed that many of these people died due to the overcrowding conditions of the old cells. It is believed that not all of the restless souls that died in the jail have moved on. Some of the spirits of the prisoners are apparently spiteful. Construction workers reported that during remodeling of the tea shop, bricks were spotted flying through the air at the workmen's heads.

The Old West Paranormal team investigated the historic jail and captured some interesting evidence. One photo showed a very dark shadowy figure hovering in a corner of the hallway near the jail cells. They have recorded unexplained sounds of knocks responding on command and the clicking sound of shackles used to restrain the prisoners. They were also able to capture recordings of names of possible ghostly inmates during their late night EVP sessions.

Owner Christina Williams noted, "Over the years, the jail was abandoned and transformed into a variety of different venues before settling on its current occupants—the tea and cupcake house—the Wild Rose. Since the opening of the Wild Rose, there have been reports of shadows, often in the shape of humans, moving about the teahouse without any proper reasoning."

Although the bootlegging ghosts of the Wild Rose Tea House may have done time in the old jail for smuggling illegal liquors, they will have to settle for a bit of "tea-totaling" these days when they come to haunt their old cells.

Wild Rose of Historic Old Town Tea House
1101 N Main St.
Cottonwood, AZ 86326
928-649-0056
www.wildrosetea.net

Crown King Saloon & Cafe, Crown King

History

The Crown King Saloon & Café has been in operation for over 100 years and is one of Arizona's oldest bars. One version of its history states that the building operated as a mining saloon in the town of Alexandra until around 1895. When that mine played out, the saloon was dismantled board by board and reconstructed in the town of Oro Belle. Other references indicate the saloon was originally built in Oro Belle in 1898, so we may never know its real origin.

Frank Morgan relocated the saloon to Crown King in 1916, transporting it up the steep pathways of Crown King Road by mules. The first operator of the reborn saloon was Alphonso Caggiano, but Tom Anderson soon became the new proprietor. Anderson was reared in Tennessee and came to work in the Crown King Mines in 1896. He was a carpenter and cabinet maker and constructed many of the wooden coffins during the flu epidemic of 1918. During prohibition, Anderson was said to have made moonshine and hard cider for his loyal patrons.

The eight rooms upstairs above the bar are said to have functioned as a bordello in the early years in Oro Belle. In Crown King, the upstairs was used as a boarding house. Tom's wife, Vonna Anderson, cooked meals for the miners, and Tom ran the bar until his death in 1956. Grant Van Tilborg bought the saloon and owned it until he died in 1975. It is still a popular watering hole for both residents and guests of Crown King.

Visitors can get a true picture of what life (and death) was like in the old town of Crown King by viewing several historic photographs of the area that grace the walls of the saloon.

Ghosts

Undocumented legends say that the notorious Mexican bandit and revolutionary, Pancho Villa, stopped in the saloon when he hid out in Crown King. Some say he worked as a wood chopper in the Crown King Mine in the early days and one of his favorite drinking spots was Anderson's Saloon.

The upstairs rooms are no longer "open for business," but local Crown King residents are eager to tell the story of the Crown King ghost they call "Leatherbelly." They say Leatherbelly was about 35-40 years old and was one of the "working ladies" from the upstairs brothel. Someone murdered her in Crown King, but nobody knows her real name. From time to time she likes to make her presence known. Call ahead—on occasion guests are allowed to pay for an overnight stay in one of the seven "upstairs" rooms. Room number 7 is said to be haunted by Leatherbelly.

Leatherbelly has often been seen in the upstairs bathroom. One guest reported he dropped the soap in the shower. He bent over to pick up the soap and noticed a scantily dressed middle-aged woman out of the corner of his eye. Other guests have seen her "reflection" in the bathroom mirror.

A gentleman on the "Ghost Sightings" blog professed to being one of the former cooks in the café in the back of the saloon. He also lived upstairs, above the establishment, in Room #6. He often heard whispers and people talking from down below. He heard sounds of a party going on—along with the sound of chairs being moved around. Startled at the possibility of intruders, he would go downstairs and find the door securely latched and no party revelers in sight.

His first night there he heard a voice. "Where is Anna?" the disembodied voice asked in the darkness. He looked around and saw no one. He was the only person in the building. His last night there he saw an elderly woman silently floating over his bed. He screamed for it to get the hell away from him. He shot across the bed, hit the wall and continued to yell at the ghost to go away. It finally dissipated into thin air. The cook worked in the café for about two months and witnessed many things he could not explain.

Of course there are also a few other ghostly spirits bellying up to the bar with the distilled spirits downstairs in the Crown King Saloon. One of the guests was sitting alone at the end of the bar one Saturday night sipping on a bottle of beer. It was very late and no one else was in the bar except the bartender on the other side of the building. The man became bewildered when suddenly a loud sound of crumpling paper occurred right next to his seat. Nobody had an explanation for the mysterious phenomena. Residents often joke that the spirits of Crown King like to have fun with the city folk who come to visit— just like they did back in the day on a lively Saturday night.

The Crown King Saloon & Café
7219 Main St.
Crown King, AZ 86343
928-632-7053
www.crownkingsaloon.com

The Asylum, Jerome

History

High on a hill overlooking the town of Jerome sits the stately Jerome Grand Hotel. This ominous structure was built on a 50 degree mountain slope. It is five stories high and 30,000 square feet of what was once the United Verde Hospital. It opened its doors in 1927, and by 1930 it had become one of the best equipped hospitals in Arizona. The basement still boasts the original Kewanee boiling system, which is in working order and heats the building today.

When Jerome's mining operations shut down, the population of this once thriving city decreased as well. The hospital closed in the 1950's. It was placed on standby conditions, becoming an "on-call" facility to be used in case a major tragedy or viral outbreak should happen. Eventually the town became deserted and the doors to the hospital were locked for good. Jerome had suddenly become a real ghost town.

The menacing-looking building lay vacant for years, decaying like the other structures in Jerome. Creative craftsmen and artists moved into the town and purchased the run-down houses for little or no money. Sometimes transients found the old hospital a perfect refuge from the cold in the winter and heat in the summer. The children in town found it an interesting place to explore and play in. Soon the windows were broken, the paint was peeling, and the building had fallen into disrepair.

In 1994, Phelps Dodge sold the building to its current owner, Larry Altherr, and renovations were underway. After two long years, the hospital took on a new agenda. It was now the Jerome Grand Hotel. The sunny hotel rooms are former hospital rooms. The doors to the rooms are still wide enough to roll a hospital bed through after surgery. The dining room of the Asylum Restaurant was once the entrance and lobby area of the old hospital where the sick and healthy both mingled in another time.

Through a set of wide doors you will find yourself inside the "Asylum Restaurant and Lounge." Grab a table near a window and see panoramic sights of the Verde Valley, Sedona, and Flagstaff. The Asylum is a restaurant definitely on the fringe.

Ghosts

In 2005, the MVD Ghostchasers held a second Spirit Workshop in Jerome. We decided to book several rooms at the Jerome Grand Hotel for a night of investigating. Debe sat on the steps of the Jerome Grand awaiting the arrival of the workshop guests when she received an exciting phone call. A local movie producer was making a documentary called "Spirits of Jerome" that weekend, and he invited the workshop crew to be a part of the filming. They had access to several of the old buildings in and around Jerome, including the Jerome Grand Hotel's basement.

As the workshop guests began to arrive, we ordered iced tea on the outside patio of the Asylum. There were filming waivers to sign, and the excitement of the group was contagious—probably a good thing we were staying at the old hospital. We posed for our group picture on the steps that lead into the Asylum dining room. The group registered at the Jerome Grand Hotel desk and started to uncover some of the mysteries of the building.

Kevin Grubb had been an employee at the Asylum Restaurant for nearly seven years. He told our group he had witnessed many strange things happening in the restaurant, including seeing a couple of spirits from time to time.

"The first time I was walking through the kitchen alone taking out the trash," Kevin told us, "Suddenly, I saw a man appear and disappear right in front of my eyes. He was peeking around a corner and looked me straight in the eye."

"Do you remember what he looked like?" we inquired.

"He had a twisted smile and wore a blue work shirt," Kevin recalled, "His hair was stringy and he had a sharp hook-like nose. I had to walk right past him which really creeped me out! Since then, I have met a lot of guests in the restaurant who have seen him too!"

Tucson author Billie Brannock was visiting Jerome and decided to walk up to the Jerome Grand Hotel. It was late in the evening and the restaurant had already closed for the night. She was standing at the north end of the Grand in front of the Asylum, and snapped a picture of what looked like a nurse standing on the outside patio balcony. She said the apparition had a white nursing cap upon her head. She looked dark from the waist up and white from the waist down. Both arms reached down and out. It seemed she was holding the hand of a small child with her right hand and a basket of supplies with her left hand. She had no feet and her face was indiscernible.

A gentleman seated at a dining room table excused himself to use the men's room. While he was washing his hands, he turned to admire an old ironing board displayed along the wall in the restroom. Suddenly, the faucet turned off by itself. At first he thought it was an automatic censored faucet system. But after turning the faucets on and off by hand several times, he declared the faucets were operating on their own.

I received an email from a couple of ghost hunters who were spending the weekend at the Jerome Grand Hotel. Roman and Candace came down to the Asylum for dinner and found a table with a fabulous view of the Verde Valley. Candace raised an eyebrow and announced she had felt something touch her leg. They took some infrared thermometer readings and discovered the temperature was between 32-45 degrees. Everywhere else near the table was over 62-65 degrees. Was there an unseen guest seated at their table?

My very intuitive friend, Cap, spent a relaxing weekend at the Jerome Grand a couple of years ago. He had gone down to the Asylum for dinner and drinks and found a cozy corner to study the dinner menu. After ordering, he excused himself and headed to the hallway toward the restroom facilities. As he glanced down the hallway, he experienced a psychic vision that lasted several seconds. What he "saw" in his mind's eye was a room full of people—doctors, nurses, and patients from another dimension bustling around in what looked like an emergency room. We learned he had been walking near the old emergency room area of the hospital. He was simply witnessing a scene from another time period as the hospital received another trauma victim.

One of the ex-bartenders of the Asylum shared an experience he witnessed as the spiritual veil grew thin in the month of October one year. It was a weekday evening in Jerome. It had snowed earlier that day and all was still and quiet. Not a breeze stirred the air. Only the cook, a waitress, one guest, and the bartender were present in the restaurant. The cook was busy in the kitchen while the waitress and bartender chatted with the lone guest in the dining room.

Suddenly the front door burst open and a large steady wall of wind whirled into the dining room. It headed past the greeter stand and threw a novelty Halloween decoration skeleton up into the air—which would not be very surprising unless the bartender described what happened next. The skeleton literally walked along the ceiling for several feet, then walked down the side of a nearby pole, eventually landing on the floor below.

The cook entered the dining room—his face pale after describing running into the wall of wind out in the hallway. The blast of wind had rushed down the corridor on its way to the where the emergency trauma room once was located.

The employees looked at each other in disbelief. Once again everything had become still and quiet on that snowy Jerome evening, but they knew they had encountered a ghost or energy field of perhaps some tragic emergency of the past.

While visiting Jerome, look for the blinking "Vacancy" sign at the Jerome Grand Hotel and drive up the narrow road to the old hospital. The Asylum Restaurant has lunch, dinner and wine guaranteed to get you on your feet again. Grab a table near a window and enjoy the breathtaking views. It's like taking a dose of tranquility. However, don't go to the Asylum if you are not ready to encounter one of the ghosts. That would be just crazy!

The Asylum Restaurant/Jerome Grand Hotel
200 Hill St.
Jerome, AZ 86331
928-639-3197
www.theasylum.biz

The Haunted Hamburger, Jerome

History

The Jerome Palace/Haunted Hamburger building was constructed in 1908 and once was a boarding house for miners working
for the United Verde Mining Company. The four floor structure
was known as the WyKoff Apartments and owned by an attorney
residing in Prescott, Arizona. Three men would share one room as
they rotated their eight hour mining shifts. It was later used as a
private residence in the 1940's where a family of three generations
shared the quarters until the 1970's. The bottom two floors is still
a residence today.

In the 1970's, the building was converted into a restaurant
called The Jerome Palace, which is where they get their current
local name—combining "The Palace" and "Haunted Hamburger."
The Haunted Hamburger is a family-owned restaurant that opened
in May of 1994. Everyone visiting the town of Jerome merely has
to follow the aroma of the charcoaled burgers to locate the Jerome
Palace Haunted Hamburger establishment. Paranormal experts
love good food as well as dining at locations known for a haunt or
two. The Haunted Hamburger satisfies both of these needs.

Ghosts

The hauntings began several years ago when Michelle and Eric
Jurisin acquired the building. It was old, abandoned, and needed
a lot of repairs before they could open as a restaurant to feed the
hungry tourists of Jerome.

Sometimes when renovations or changes are made in old buildings, the spirits return to observe these updates and greet the new
occupants. The spirits of the Haunted Hamburger were no excep-
tion. As soon as tradesmen began converting the building into one

of the finest eating establishments of Jerome, mysterious things began to happen. Tools began to disappear on a regular basis. First one hammer—then two—then three hammers had vanished! Some carpenters found themselves not very comfortable working on the job site with a ghost around.

At first the Jurisins figured they were just setting the hammers down and forgetting where they had placed them. But after a former owner asked if they had met the ghosts and warned them about the mysterious disappearance of hammers, they knew they had become the latest victims of the prankster ghost. Soon after, the hammers started to reappear—one by one—in the most visible places. Sometimes the hammers were found in a heaping pile in the attic.

While Eric Jurison was in the middle of this restoration project, he remembered he needed to go back upstairs to complete a task he had started earlier that day. Just as he reached the top floor, the door that he was standing next to slammed, nearly smashing him in the face. One might think a crosswind is strong enough to slam a door, and would be perfectly right. Except, Eric had just sealed up all the windows in the building with thick, heavy-duty plastic and duct tape to keep the cold winter air out. He knew there was no way an air current could have blown through the securely winterized building.

The owners and staff have witnessed the slamming of doors, lights flickering on and off, and bottles and glasses flying off of sturdy shelves. Some have seen shadows or felt cold breezes of unseen guests dashing past them in the rooms or on the staircase. A mysterious image of a woman has been photographed by various paranormal groups and visiting photographers.

The Arizona Paranormal Research Society conducted an investigation at the Haunted Hamburger in August 2007. The team set up cameras and equipment throughout the building using the patio area as their base camp. One member of the group snapped a photo of what looked like a man peering back at him. Once the photo was adjusted for brightness and contrast you could almost make out the facial features. EVP sessions were held in the upstairs dining room, but no class 1 EVP's were recorded.

Next time you are in Jerome, stop at the Haunted Hamburger. The Ghostly Burger is one of the favorite meals, the view of the valley is spectacular, and you just might be seated with a ghost. Oh, and you might want to leave your tool belt out in your vehicle.

Haunted Hamburger
410 N Clark St.
Jerome, AZ 86331
928-634-0554
www.thehauntedhamburger.com

Mile High Grill, Jerome

History

J. H. Clinkscale, an insurance adjuster from Los Angeles, California built the two-story structure that houses the Mile High Inn and Grill in Jerome after one of several devastating fires raged through the town in 1899. The building is listed on the National Register of Historic Places. This was the third time the town, primarily built of wooden structures, had been consumed by flames in two years. Clinkscale wanted his new building to be fireproof, so he had it constructed using reinforced concrete, with walls measuring eighteen inches thick. Thanks to its sturdy construction, the new building did not burn down, and it never faltered during the endless dynamite blasting in the mines that caused some establishments across the street to slide down the hillside.

Originally, the building was a hardware store on the lower level with offices upstairs. It has since held other businesses such as the Owen & Nevin Undertaking Parlor, a bordello, a candy store, and now the Mile High Inn and Grill. Once known as the "Wickedest Town in the West" during its heyday, Jerome was anything but the peaceful art community it is today. It was a wild and violent mining town—even more so than the notorious Tombstone—where the ruthless code of the Old West was in effect. The building's history appropriately contains pieces of that unlawful past.

Jennie Bauters is sometimes credited with being Jerome's first madam. Jennie, who operated her business upstairs in what is now the Mile High Inn and Grill at the turn of the 20th century, went on to be the most popular madam and one of the richest women in Arizona. Jennie was later murdered in 1905 on the streets, at Acme Camp near Gold Road in Mohave County (near the town of Kingman), by a man named Clement C. Leigh.

The building was updated in 1994, and the eatery was renovated to its current character. Ghosts from bygone years stir in these walls, hinting at the secrets and memories still buried within. The business was purchased by Liz Gale, and re-opened its doors as the Mile High Inn and Grill in 2004. It has become a local favorite, providing a safe, relaxing place to dine or a great night spot to unwind.

Ghosts

The Mile High Grill has had its share of ghostly mischief throughout the years. Glasses tend to fall off the tables when no one is around to be held responsible. Waitstaff members actually witnessed a glass on the countertop slide across the surface by itself and crash to the floor.

While one of the cooks was bending over to grab a bowl underneath the prep table, two plastic containers on the top storage shelf fell, hitting him in the back of the head. He was alone in the kitchen, and shaken by the incident. Luckily the containers were made of plastic and empty at the time.

Early one morning before opening, a cook heard what sounded like someone in the building whistling. A waitress was in the restroom washing her hands. Although she did not hear the whistling, she did hear a female voice singing and then a loud bang. Assuming the cook had the radio blaring loud, she entered the kitchen and realized that the radio had not been turned on and the cook had not dropped anything to make the sound she had heard. On the same note, the cook had not heard the singing nor the bang. Keep in mind that the building's reinforced eighteen-inch concrete walls hinder normal acoustics; sound does not travel far. So even if someone had been whistling, singing, or playing the radio, it is not likely that people in different rooms would have heard these sounds.

It is believed there could be as many as four ghosts that haunt the Mile High Inn and Grill: Jennie Bauters, the madam of the bordello; an elderly man seen in the hallways; a younger man who loves pulling pranks; and a spirited cat nick-named Sipps who loves to nestle and nip at your ankles.

The Mile High Grill's atmosphere reflects on Jerome's small-town culture. The tables at the window nooks overlook Main Street and are ideal for people-watching…or perhaps ghost watching. But then again, perhaps the spirits will be watching you!

The Mile High Grill
309 Main St.
Jerome, AZ 86331
928-634-5094
www.milehighgrillandinn.com

Vaqueros Grill & Cantina aka Red Rooster Café, Jerome

History

The structure housing the Red Rooster Café (now the Vaqueros Grill & Cantina), built in 1920, was once a popular grocery store called "Pay and Take It." During the 1930's, Safeway Stores bought the business out, and for a while the Jerome franchise was the smallest store in their chain. The building was abandoned in the 1950's when mining ceased and folks moved away from Jerome. The roof fell in and the front of the building collapsed. In the 1970's, the building was bought and restored to its former glory. If you look very closely, you can still make out the painted signs "Safeway" and "Pay n' Take It" on the brickwork above the front door. The building has since been an ice cream parlor and a restaurant. Joe and Peter are the third owners. It is listed on the National Register of Historic Places.

Ghosts

There are several rumors on the origin of the name Red Rooster Café. The story told to me was that a rooster used to frequent the vacant 'street artist' lot next door. A patron of the old ice cream parlor stated that the people living in the nearby apartments were annoyed by the constant crowing noise of the aggressive rooster and waking them far too early in the morning. Someone decided to put a stop to the racket and blasted the old rooster with a shotgun. Today, down near the Jerome Gallery, a rooster and gaggle of hens will sometimes block traffic. Could one of their ancestors be haunting the Red Rooster Café?

Joe and Peter completely rebuilt the kitchen of the café in the spring of 2008, and speculated that during that process, something might have been disturbed.

A former waitress by the name of Brenda was on a ladder adjusting the positions of several wine bottles on a shelf. Earlier, she had placed an almost empty plastic cup next to her on the bar. She looked down to see the cup rise up and drop to the floor six feet away from her. She also claimed that one night she heard rustling upstairs in the dry storage area above the kitchen. Thinking that the cook was still in the building, she went upstairs but found no one in sight. Who or whatever was there in the café seemed to enjoy playing pranks on Brenda. Bending over as she reached into a cupboard one evening, Brenda swore something bumped into her. Could it have been a ghost? Brenda claimed it was very small in size. Perhaps rooster-sized.

Being a skeptic, the owner placed oatmeal on the floor and watched it for long periods of time. Nothing ever happened. However, when left overnight and observed the following morning, the little pile of oatmeal would be spread around. Could the ghost really be a case of mice? But, wouldn't mortal mice eat the oatmeal laid out before them?

Deb Wilber of Verde Valley Spirit Seekers and I were asked to come up to Jerome and investigate the Red Rooster Café and perhaps dig into the history of the rooster theory.

After a delightful lunch to sort of get the feel of the place, Joe took us up the staircase in the back of the café to the second level where all the ghostly action was said to take place. We took a few photographs and decided to do a little experiment. We took a handful of oatmeal and placed it on the ground. Then we took a piece of white chalk and drew a circle around the "bait." We asked the owner to report back to us in the morning if the oatmeal had been moved. We offered to come back and bring our full paranormal teams to do an overnight investigation if the ghostly rooster persisted in tormenting the employees.

After a bit of research we learned that the adjoining building to the café was once a butcher/meat processing shop. Here beef, pork and even chicken were prepared for sale to local consumers. One could guess that the former grocery stores purchased these fresh meat items to pass on to their patrons. Is the ghostly rooster a residual spirit seeking revenge of the 'fowl' play when its life was cut so short?

Joe showed us where the alleged rooster and his following of devoted hens were seen in the streets and the overhang near the English Kitchen where they were said to take shelter now and then. Not a single "poultry-geist" was in sight!

The Red Rooster Café is no longer open in Jerome, Arizona. It is now known as Vaqucro's.

Vaqueros Grill & Cantina
363 S Main St.
Jerome, AZ 86331
928-649-9090
www.vaquerosgrill.org

Matt's Longhorn Saloon, Prescott

History

During the summer heat wave that can boil your tap water and fry eggs on the sidewalk, a lot of ghost hunters travel north where the temperatures are not as torrid. One of the more popular cities in which to encounter a ghost is Prescott, Arizona, and that's where Matt's Longhorn Saloon can quench your thirst for ghosts and a sarsaparilla.

The original building was constructed in the 1870's and was a busy mercantile store. The store was destroyed in the July 1900 fire that snuffed out most of the booming businesses along Whisky Row. Rebuilt in 1901, the historic D. Levy Building housed the mercantile until 1934. Prohibition had come to an end, and the store was replaced by a saloon.

The swinging wooden doors of Matt's Longhorn Saloon have been a fixture on Whisky Row since 1962. Longhorn skulls and mounted game decorate the walls of the saloon. A twenty-foot-long bar front invites guests to "belly up to the bar" to order their favorite drink, while a large wooden dance floor attracts two-step country-western dancers on the weekends.

Ghosts

The owners, plus some employees and guests, have witnessed the ghosts left behind in the saloon. Most frequently seen is a tall dark figure of a cowboy, usually wearing his black duster and hat as though he just returned from a trail ride. He lingers in the establishment late at night waiting to be served one more drink before his last call is announced.

Another spirit noted at the saloon is that of a little girl. She has been seen in the ladies' restroom asking for someone to help her find her mother. Alarmed employees and guests report they have mistaken the spirit for a missing child. Before they are able to assist the young girl, she has vanished before their eyes.

Paranormal investigation teams have recorded EVP of both the cowboy and a female voice, so if you are in the saloon late on a quiet night, your recorder might pick up on a disembodied voice. The Arizona Desert Ghost Hunters reported hearing what sounded like a marble rolling from the men's room to the pool table along the wooden floor. They all followed the sound with their eyes and ears as the hair stood up on their arms and neck.

Stop in at Matt's Saloon on Whisky Row and keep an eye on your barstool. You never know who might be keeping you company.

Matt's Longhorn Saloon
112 S Montezuma St.
Prescott, AZ 86303
928-771-8788
www.mattssaloon.com

The Palace Saloon, Prescott

History

The Palace Saloon opened in Prescott, Arizona in September 1877. Prescott's Whisky Row sported a number of saloons, but the Palace was much more than your average honky-tonk or watering hole establishment. It was decked out in grand style and only the finest liqueurs from around the world were served. The Palace was the gathering point where men checked the boards for available work, came for the news of local and national election results, and conducted mineral claim business over the bar.

A fire in 1883 destroyed several of the buildings on Whisky Row, including the original Palace. Owner Robert Brow made the decision to rebuild his popular drinking establishment stronger and grander than before. The new Palace Saloon had a stone foundation and sturdy brick walls. Inside, a 20-foot-long bar with an ornate back bar accented the new saloon.

Unfortunately, another fire ignited in July of 1900, which destroyed much of downtown Prescott. Even the Palace Saloon could not be saved. They say saloon patrons grabbed the liquor inventory and delivered it across the street to the courthouse plaza. The beautiful 1880's Brunswick bar was hoisted up by the faithful customers and carried to safety at the plaza as well. Drinks were served to the thirsty men as the blaze devastated the city.

The present Palace saloon reopened as the Palace Hotel in June 1901. It was a two story masonry building with a Neo-Classical Revival design. It was built of gray granite, iron, and pressed ornamental bricks. Near the top of the front façade is a carved seal of the Territory of Arizona. The hotel sported large gambling tables that included faro, poker, roulette, keno and craps. A man could pay for his drinks with un-minted gold. The Palace had hostesses who entertained with music—and possibly a bit of prostitution was served on the side.

More recently, movie producers have come to love the location, and films like "Junior Bonner" with Steve McQueen and "Billy Jack" used the Palace in some memorable movie scenes. In 1996, new owners took over the Palace Saloon and major restoration began. With the aid of old photos, the beauty and elegance of the palace Hotel and Saloon of 1901 was again recaptured.

Ghosts

The Arizona-based MVD Ghostchasers paranormal team has had the pleasure of dining and ghost hunting at the historical Palace Saloon on several occasions. Once, the team was in Prescott doing a feature newspaper story on the haunted town. After several hours of doing mini investigations at local business and hotels, we decided a relaxing dinner at the Palace was in order.

While waiting for our meals to arrive at the table, we asked about the legendary ghosts still stepping up to the bar to quench their thirst. Our EMF meter began to show a reading about 2.2 near the back of the dining area—then suddenly subsided back to 0.5, an average reading.

I was curious to learn what went on in that back area. Our waitress told us a story of a high-stakes poker game played in the Palace. A man named Nevins was in debt; he put his mortuary up as collateral. Legend says the ill-fated poker game was played in the back of the Palace Saloon. The men sat down at a poker table and the cards were carefully shuffled. Tension filled the room. A large crowd assembled as the two men played for the rights of ownership of the funeral parlor. Nevins lost everything he owned to the sheriff. Perhaps his spirit returns to the poker room to replay that fateful game of cards.

Owner Dave Michelson was happy to share some of his ghost stories with us. He presented a photograph of the bar from the 1890's that showed what looked like a ghostly figure in the background. Eyes widened as we studied the photo. He told us glasses fall off the rack for no reason, and once a plant that had been sitting on the bar for quite a spell suddenly fell to the ground.

Another time a mannequin dressed in period clothing fell over the railing at the top of the stairs. There was no one around the staircase at the time.

As in most haunted saloons, bottles, glasses, mugs and other items tend to move about the bar front on their own, leaving the bartenders and wait staff in a state of confusion.

In the movie "Junior Bonner," a raging fight scene was filmed in the sprawling barroom of the Palace. It was one of the largest saloon brawls captured on film. Chairs and people were flying in every direction and crashing onto the tables. Bottles were thrown and the sound of glass breaking filled the Palace from one end to the other. Could the prankster ghosts be cowboys of an earlier time, or just one of the movie cowboys playing out a Peckinpah scene?

The Palace Restaurant and Saloon
120 S Montezuma
Prescott, AZ 86303
928-541-1996
www.historicpalace.com

Rock Springs Café, Rock Springs

History

The Rock Springs Café, located 45 miles north of Phoenix, Arizona, was established in 1918. Heading north, travelers find the landscape beginning to change from barren desert to plateaus and mountains. The eponymous springs once served as a watering hole for trappers, cowboys and US Army soldiers.

Rock Springs was merely a Black Canyon Stagecoach stop between Prescott and Phoenix beginning in 1884. A strong box currently hanging from the ceiling in the café was aboard the last stage run in 1917. Legends say that many notorious characters from the Old West have stopped along the trail at Rock Springs, including Morgan and Wyatt Earp and Doc Holliday.

In 1918, Ben Warner settled on the land, naming the location and his business Rock Springs. By 1920 he was running a small canvas-covered general store selling groceries and mining supplies. A new general store, hotel and saloon graced the site in 1924. The building was constructed of concrete blocks—each block having the imprint of a cowboy boot heel. You can still see some of those original blocks in the dining room today.

The hotel has housed many notable guests as well as providing shelter to those traveling to mine the silver and gold in the Bradshaw Mountains. Western film star Tom Mix is said to have had a secret tryst with actress Jean Harlow at the hotel. Jane Russell, along with many other celebrities, drove from the Phoenix area to the Rock Springs Hotel to enjoy a quiet, romantic weekend getaway.

The seven-room hotel has since been converted into office space. Having started as one of the first general stores in Arizona, it is now one of the ten still in existence today.

Ghosts

Today the café and its famous pies are what attract the guests as they travel along I17. A variety of antiques are on display throughout the restaurant and saloon including an old copper distilling tank that flourished during the prohibition years. Some employees believe there are a few supernatural spirits who inhabit the "Rock."

The bartender at the Rock Springs Café is a longtime employee and has seen her share of 'spirits' in the old building. One night after closing, she was carefully counting out the cash drawer. She happened to look up at the doorway to the lobby from the bar entrance. At that time there were old-fashioned swinging barroom doors that graced the entry. The doors opened midway—and stayed in that position for several moments as though some unseen entity was holding them ajar. She stared at a smoky presence filtering into the room. It quickly appeared…then slowly faded away.

One morning, the kitchen chef began prepping food for the breakfast guests that arrive early and fill the restaurant each day. The frazzled cook came running into the barroom clutching a butcher knife in his hand, ranting about something that was terrorizing him in the kitchen. The bartender walked back into the kitchen with the cook and witnessed pots and pans flying off the shelves and crashing down to the floor.

The former hotel on the second floor of the building is sometimes used as a crash pad for the staff if the evening's activities get overextended. The bartender, having stayed for an afterhours event, decided to spend the night in one of the upstairs rooms rather than drive all the way home to Mesa, seventy miles away. At some point in the night, she woke up and saw a misty presence in the room. She could not make out any details, but it seemed to be that smoky filter once again. Spooked, she jumped up immediately and drove back to Mesa at 4:00 in the morning.

Other ghost tales include faucets turning on and off by themselves and toilets flushing on their own in the barroom bathroom. The cash drawer has been known to open on its own. The bartender has sensed someone standing behind her and felt someone touch the back of her shoulder. Chairs in the adjoining barroom have been knocked over from the table as if some invisible barroom fight is erupting.

Stop in at the Rock Springs Cafe, have a slice of one of their famous pies, and be on the lookout for ghostly travelers of the past.

Rock Springs Café
35769 S Old Black Canyon Hwy.
Black Canyon City, AZ 85324
623-374-5794
www.rocksprings.cafe

Basics for Ghost Hunting

Courtesy

Make sure you have permission to be on the property. Do not trespass for any reason. Act like you would in your great grandparents' house. Remember, a ghost calls its place "home" because he/she likes it or can't leave it. Respect it—don't destroy it.

Knowledge

Know what you might encounter. There are generally two types of spirits you may bump into. One was a human at one time and has remained back on Earth for some reason. It may not know it is dead, or may have stayed behind due to unfinished business, guilt, etc. These ghosts are like the person they were when alive—they could be good or bad, just like the living—but normally not dangerous! These are the sort of spirits you will encounter 99% of the time.

The other type of spirit you may encounter was never human and is generally bad news! Be aware of this sort of spirit but do not become obsessed with them. The chances you will ever encounter them in a regular ghost hunt is very slim.

You could also witness a residual haunting which is merely a playback of a past event—like watching the same DVD over and over again.

Basic Tools

Preparation

— Flashlight
— Digital Camera
— First aid kit
— Watch
— Notepad and pen
— Video Camera
— Audio Recorder
— EMF Detector
— Cell Phone
— Compass
— Motion Detector
— Thermal Scanner

○ Enter the location and either privately or as a group ask for blessing or protection for the duration of the hunt. This takes less than 30 seconds. This will put yourself in a positive frame of mind and help to keep you safe.

○ Walk around the area to get a feel for the surroundings and allow the spirits to get a feel for you. Log in the date, start time and weather conditions. Use your EMF meters to locate any false readings.

○ No smoking, drinking or drugs at any investigation for obvious reasons.

○ No whispering, as it can taint your EVP recordings. Keep talking to a minimum.

○ Be skeptical and look for alternative causes for any phenomenon such as natural or man-made sources. Make sure your final evidence will stand up to scrutiny. Always disprove before you prove, and you will be successful.

○ Always let someone know where you will be ghost hunting in case of an emergency.

○ Learn the history of the location. Read old newspapers, talk with historians, visit archive libraries which will be helpful finding history, folklore and facts about the site.

Ghost Hunting Protocol

Rules

○ Never go ghost hunting alone.

○ Always let someone know where you will be.

○ Always carry ID.

○ Always have a cell phone for emergencies.

○ If you feel uncomfortable, leave!

○ Get permission before going onto private property or to be in a cemetery after hours.

○ Reschedule your outdoor ghost hunt if it is going to snow, rain, or if it is foggy. Also check the pollen count. Moisture and pollen can cause anomalies in photos.

○ If you have a large group, break up into pairs or smaller groups.

○ Carry walkie-talkies or cell phones to communicate with fellow ghost investigators when working in remote areas.

○ Don't use drugs or alcohol before or during an investigation or hunt.

○ Don't smoke near where you will be investigating. You don't want to photograph smoke and think it is an ecto mist or spirit.

○ Never whisper when trying to record EVP. Talk in a normal voice. You won't scare the ghosts if you talk. And you don't want to mistake a human whisper for that of a spirit.

○ Always use new tapes in an analog recorder.

○ Have extra batteries and make sure all equipment is fully charged.

○ Wear a watch so you can note times of events.

○ Wear clothing suited for the weather and always wear comfortable shoes.

○ Don't wear jackets with string ties. The ties could get in the way when taking photos and be mistaken for something paranormal, especially if you are shooting downward.

○ Don't wear perfume or cologne while ghost hunting. If using an insect repellent, make sure it is unscented. Some have noticed scents or smells when there is reported ghost activity. Perfumes may mask these scents.

○ Tie back long hair. When a piece of hair gets in front of the camera lens it will look like a vortex.

○ Remove camera straps or be aware where they are when taking a photo. Many times straps get in the picture and can be mistaken for a vortex, ecto, moving orb or ghosts.

○ Look for things in the way like spider webs, wire, ropes, tree limbs. They can appear on photos as something paranormal when they are in close range of the camera lens.

○ Always clean camera lenses. Lint, dust specks, smudges and fingerprints can look like ecto mist, orbs, and other ghostly anomalies.

○ Be aware of the temperature when photographing outdoors or in an unheated building. Hold your breath while taking a photo and for several seconds afterward. Remember, if you can see it, so can the camera.

○ Always know where your fingers are when taking photos. A thumb or finger can appear to be a ghost when caught in front of the lens. It is a big letdown to find out it's not paranormal after all.

○ Research the location. If you are going ghost hunting after dark, you should check it out during daylight hours. Make note of any dangers such as holes, broken glass, loose boards etc.

○ Be objective of your findings. Rule out any natural causes that may have caused anomalies such as insects, lights in the distance, spider webs, or reflections.

○ Some believe in saying a closing prayer of protection according to your religious beliefs. We usually say something like "In the name of God we command you to stay here. Do not follow us".

○ The most important tip of all: always respect the dead.

About the Author

Debe Branning has been the director of the MVD Ghostchasers of Mesa/Bisbee paranormal team since 1995. The team conducts investigations of haunted historical locations throughout Arizona. For the past fifteen years, she has led Paranormal Workshops which provide experienced ghost hunters, paranormal team members, and folks wanting to try the art of ghost hunting a chance to work and learn techniques together. Debe has been a guest lecturer at Ottawa University, Central Arizona College, Arizona State University, and South Mountain Community College. She has been a speaker at SciFi Conventions such as CopperCon, FiestaCon, HauntedCon, AZParaCon and Phoenix ComiCon. She appeared in an episode of "Streets of Fear" for FearNet.com and an episode of Travel Channel's "Ghost Stories" about haunted Jerome, Arizona in 2010. Debe is the author of *Sleeping With Ghosts—A Ghost Hunter's Guide to AZ's Haunted Hotels and Inns, The Graveyard Shift—Arizona's Historic and Haunted Cemeteries, Grand Canyon Ghost Stories—Spooky Tales About Grand Canyon National Park* and two children's books. She pens two columns for Examiner.com titled "Arizona Haunted Sites" and "Haunted Places" so travelers will know where they might find a ghost or two when they visit Arizona and other places across the United States. Debe is a REIKI Master and a dowser. She volunteers with the Pioneers' Cemetery Association and helps organize fundraisers for gravestone preservation.